S0-AIH-841

LOW ACHIEVING CHILDREN:

The First Seven Years

Sarah Broman
Ellen Bien
Peter Shaughnessy

LOW ACHIEVING CHILDREN:

The First Seven Years

Sarah Broman
Ellen Bien
Peter Shaughnessy

LAWRENCE ERLBAUM ASSOCIATES, PUBLISHERS
1985 Hillsdale, New Jersey London

Lawrence Erlbaum Associates, Inc., Publishers
365 Broadway
Hillsdale, New Jersey 07642

Library of Congress Cataloging in Publication Data

Broman, Sarah H.
Low achieving children.

Bibliography: p.
Includes index.
1. Learning disabilities—United States. I. Bien, Ellen. II. Shaughnessy, Peter. III. Title.
LC4705.B76 1985 371.92′6 85-4443
ISBN 0-89859-637-8

Printed in the United States of America
10 9 8 7 6 5 4 3 2 1

Contents

Foreword

The Collaborative Perinatal Project was conceived as a massive humanitarian effort to provide a scientific basis "to increase the likelihood of the birth of healthy babies free from disease and impairment, and capable of optimal physical and intellectual development" (Niswander & Gordon, 1972). This book is another in a series of major reports on the outcome of the project that have documented the problems that interfere with achieving both these goals.

The goal of determining the biomedical causes of a variety of developmental disorders thought to have their roots in the perinatal period was captured in the original title of the program, the Collaborative Study of Cerebral Palsy, Mental Retardation, and Other Neurological and Sensory Disorders of Infancy and Childhood. The implicit hypothesis was that there would be fairly direct linear relationships between specific medical events and these disorders. On the basis of this rationale, funding was acquired to recruit for the study over 50,000 families from 14 different medical centers scattered around the country, and to monitor the development of children born to these families until they were seven years of age.

The first major report of the developmental outcomes was the analysis of the IQ-scores of the sample when the children were four years old (Broman, Nichols, & Kennedy, 1975). The effects on intelligence of 169 prenatal, delivery, infant, and family variables were examined in that volume. The implicit causal hypotheses of the collaborative study were reflected in this set of measures. Of the 169 variables examined, only eight were related to family characteristics. The remaining 161 were assessments of the medical and developmental condition of the mother and child through the first year of life. The surprising result of the four-year analysis is now history: The intellectual outcomes for children were far better explained by the small set of *family* factors than any combination of the multitude of *biomedical* variables.

A common image of the mentally retarded is of a physically anomalous individual with bizarre motor patterns and neurological impairment evident on the most basic examinations. The irony is that children who best fit such an image, those with cerebral palsy, are very often not retarded. In contrast, the vast majority of retarded children, the psychosocial or familial etiology group, fit into a category where there are no obvious signs of physical, motor, or neurological abnormalities. Yet there remains a belief, based on the historic biomedical understanding of disease, that somewhere in these children are organic abnormalities that are the exclusive cause of their deficiencies.

The theory that developmental disabilities have organic roots arose from observations that children with mental retardation tended to have more pregnancy and birth complications than other children. The danger in drawing conclusions from these retrospective observations is that some other factor may be producing both the perinatal and the developmental problems in these children. Prospective studies have found that there is indeed such a third factor—the social environment of the child.

The report of the preschool behavior of the large sample in the collaborative project supported the findings of many other studies that followed the development of smaller groups of children who had experienced perinatal complications. If social variables are ignored, there seems to be a correlational causal connection between birth complications and later lower IQ. When social status is included in the analysis, children from poorer socioeconomic groups are found to suffer from the most perinatal difficulties and to have the lowest intelligence scores. In fact, the double burden of an adverse medical condition and an adverse social condition frequently act synergistically to worsen the fate of these children, compared with children who experienced only one of these detrimental conditions.

This volume is the second major report on the intellectual development of the children from the collaborative study. Its focus moves from the general case of mental retardation to examine the etiology of more specific learning disabilities. Children with low IQs are expected to do poorly in school. But what about children with normal intelligence who do poorly? The analysis of the development of these children was expected to offer new hope for the identification of specific biomedical causes of these school-age disorders. Where the etiology of general mental retardation does not seem to be illuminated by an analysis of the early medical condition of the child, more specific entities, such as learning disabilities, dyslexia, minimal brain dysfunction, hyperkinetic syndrome, or attention deficit disorder, might be better targets for biological causal models.

From a sample of 35,000 children tested at seven years of age in the collaborative study, approximately one thousand were identified as having normal intelligence but showing poor school performance. This cohort was compared with over 6,000 children who had normal school performance to evaluate the contribution of perinatal conditions, behavior during the preschool period, and the child's social environment to problems of learning, reading, and hyperactivity.

The most compelling result of the 7-year follow-up analysis was that even when specific conditions are studied the primary causal factors reside not in the child's biomedical history, but in the child's environment, the social context of development. "Major findings in this study support and augment the conclusions of others that lower socioeconomic status, less maternal education, higher birth order, and larger family size are related to higher rates of academic failure . . . " (p.114, this volume).

Most clinicians are familiar with cases of children who have learning or reading problems, or who cannot sit still in class and who have been unsuccessfully treated by a variety of educational therapists, only to have the parents eventually discover that their child has a brain lesion that is causing the disordered behavior. There are clearer examples of children with major neurological disorders that produce severe retardation. These cases are highly salient in determining how some scientists view these disorders. While it is clear that such cases exist, the evidence remains that for the majority of cognitively impaired children the causes lie elsewhere. The planners of the Collaborative Perinatal Project had the foresight to include a small set of social and family variables in their study. So far, these variables have provided the greatest payoff in explaining the adverse intellectual outcomes in the large sample studied.

In the 25 years since this project was designed, developmental scientists have come a long way in understanding the causes of behavioral disabilities. Sociological factors only provide a framework in which psychological factors can operate. The 4- and 7-year follow-ups of the children in the collaborative study have provided an important set of facts. Children from poor families living in crowded conditions with poorly educated parents have lower IQs and do poorly in school. It would be a mistake, however, simply to substitute the set of social factors for the previous set of medical factors as the cause of learning problems. If the ultimate goal of these studies is to provide a scientific basis for preventing learning disabilities, other factors will prove to be even more important. These factors will be discovered in studies of the process of development, of how the biological condition of the child interacts over time with the child's social condition. More specifically, such studies will be directed at the behavioral interactions between poorly educated, overstressed, and underfinanced parents and their children. To the extent that these children are also suffering from medical conditions related to their perinatal experiences, studies will be necessary to find out how these illnesses worsen social interactions or are worsened by social interactions, so that early physical disorders are transformed into later psychological ones.

The results of the collaborative project begun in the fifties provide an agenda for the eighties. A succession of studies have used increasingly refined measures to identify biological anomalies in newborn infants. The empirical results of these studies continue to be that the majority of children suffering from these conditions grow up to be children with normal IQs and normal school functioning. This empirical evidence has begun to make a mark on our theoretical understanding of child development which brings us back to the original goals of the Collaborative Perinatal Project.

The goal of increasing the "likelihood of the birth of babies free from disease and impairment" is the one toward which the most advance has been made. Our medical successes have been documented by the steady drop in the mortality rate for preterm infants in the United States as compared to the rest of the world. The ability of perinatologists to assure the physical survival of the tiniest babies has become almost commonplace. However, even in this realm our social failures are documented by the high infant mortality rate in urban areas where lack of education and poverty prevail.

The goal of producing babies capable of "optimal physical and intellectual development" (p. vii, this volume) has proven even more elusive and has required the most restructuring of our thinking. It has become increasingly evident that this goal will never be reached through medical means alone. Whereas the physical integrity of the child is a prerequisite for intellectual development, children with a wide range of physical handicaps from blindness to cerebral palsy can achieve superior levels of learning. On the other hand, it is far less likely that children with experiential handicaps will attain such levels of achievement. The limiting factors for the vast majority of children lie not in their physical condition but in the family and cultural context, that is, the inability of parents with an abundance of stresses and a paucity of resources to adequately raise their children.

Through the study of a large cohort of children, the Collaborative Perinatal Project has achieved great importance in redirecting our efforts to assure optimal intellectual growth for children. Whereas little light was shed on the etiology of rare developmental disorders, much light has been shed on the major problems that afflict children in our society. The authors of this volume have continued their important work by reinforcing the evidence for the overpowering influence of social circumstance on child development put forward in earlier analyses of the collaborative study data.

The last, but perhaps most important, issue to be raised in this Foreword may be more appropriate for an Afterword. This issue is the future of research into the causes of mental subnormality. The question is whether or not we have reached the point where the federal research investment of hundreds of millions of dollars can be directed by a new model for understanding the causes of mental retardation and school failure. In this modern view, strongly supported by the evidence of this volume, the biomedical condition of the child is only one ingredient in the psychosocial context that will determine the intellectual health of future generations.

Arnold Sameroff
Center for Advanced Study in
the Behavorial Sciences
January, 1985

Preface

This monograph is the result of the dedicated efforts of many people. It presents an assessment of the early development and later functioning of children in the Collaborative Perinatal Project who were low achievers at age seven. The primary contributions were made by the population of mothers and children who participated in the longitudinal Collaborative Project of the National Institute of Neurological and Communicative Disorders and Stroke, and the members of the multidisciplinary staffs of the 12 research centers who conducted the examinations, tests, and interviews that began in the prenatal period.

The current study involved the preparation and analysis of extensive data files and we are grateful to Mr. James Pomeroy for his responsive and efficient computer programming. Dr. Paul Nichols was an always helpful consultant and Mrs. Margaret Henney prepared the final manuscript expeditiously. We are also indebted to Dr. Jerome Kagan, Dr. Lee Willerman, and Dr. Lillian Belmont for valuable suggestions made after careful readings of an earlier version of the manuscript.

Sarah Broman
Ellen Bien
Peter Shaughnessy

1 Introduction

Children with normal aptitude or intelligence and poor school performance have been classified in many ways, depending on the profession and era of the categorist (Feagans, 1983; Mercer, Forgnone, & Wolking, 1976). This taxonomic confusion continues to cause serious concern (Cruickshank, 1983). Most frequently, these children are called learning disabled, a group that is one of the largest to receive educational services under Public Law 94–142, The Education of All Handicapped Children Act of 1975 (Dearman & Plisko, 1980). Many basic issues surrounding learning disabilities remain unresolved including those of definition, prevalence, etiology, and remediation. Prevalence estimates in school-age children range from 2 to 20% depending on the definition adopted and the samples surveyed. Apparent increases in the number of children failing to acquire basic academic skills and the expectation that the deficits will become larger with increasing age has created a sense of urgency, especially among educators. Factors contributing to the increase are changes in both educational policy and research and treatment approaches to the problems of unexpected academic difficulties.

Public schools have become more public as a result of a mandatory attendance requirement, a minimum drop-out age, and the federally supported right to appropriate education for all children. Teachers are now educating children whom they may not have found in their classrooms before. An emphasis on written forms of instruction may cause the slow reader to lag even further behind, and large-scale testing programs may identify him or her sooner and more often. New research techniques have led to an intensified search for neurophysiological and neuroanatomical substrates of cognitive processes, both normal and abnormal. A fairly widespread use of stimulant drugs to modify hyperactive-inattentive behavior in schoolchildren has reinforced acceptance of a physiological model to explain these behaviors. Finally, the area of learning disabilities has attracted the interest of pediatricians, neurologists, and psychiatrists in their efforts to treat the "whole" child.

The term learning disabilities was introduced by Samuel Kirk in 1962 to focus attention on assessment and remediation of educational deficits rather than on an assumed underlying brain injury or perceptual handicap. He (Kirk, 1962) defined a learning disability as "a retardation, disorder, or delayed development in one or more of the processes of speech, language, reading, writing, or arithmetic resulting from a possible cerebral dysfunction and/or emotional or behavioral disturbance and not from mental retardation, sensory deprivation, or cultural or instructional factors" (p. 263). Subsequent modifications of the definition of learning disabilities have involved the issues of normal intellectual ability and etiology.

Most descriptions of learning-disabled children include level of intellectual functioning as a primary marker or as an exclusion. Some investigators and theorists have required that intelligence tests scores fall in the average or above average ranges (Menkes, 1974; Mercer et al., 1976; Pannbacker, 1968; Siegel, 1968; Sulzbacher, 1975), whereas others have required only the absence of mental retardation (Kirk, 1962; Myklebust, 1968). Cruickshank (1977) disagrees with the inclusion of a minimum IQ score in the definition of a learning disability, which he believes could be present at any intellectual level. Emotional problems were excluded as an etiological factor in the Learning Disabilities Act of 1969 and this exclusion has been widely accepted. Emotional difficulties are often cited as secondary complications in learning disabilities. For example, Rutter has reported a strong association between reading retardation and conduct-disturbance disorders (Rutter, 1980; Rutter, Tizard, & Whitmore, 1970).

Beyond references to difficulties in "processing," most definitions of learning disabilities do not include specific etiological factors. Kirk and Bateman (1962) refer to a possible cerebral dysfunction and/or emotional or behavioral disturbances as underlying causes of a more immediate psychological handicap. Cruickshank (1977) views the perceptual processing deficits associated with learning disabilities as neurological phenomena. In many definitions, sensory or motor handicaps and environmental disadvantage are excluded as primary causes of learning disabilities along with mental retardation and emotional difficulties.

Clarification of what constitutes a learning disability was attempted in the final formulation of the federal rules for Public Law 94–142 published in December of 1977. Specific learning disabilities were defined as achievement incommensurate with age and ability level when appropriate learning experience has been provided, and, more specifically, as a severe discrepancy between achievement and intellectual ability in one or more of the areas of oral or written expression, listening comprehension, basic reading skill or reading comprehension, or mathematical calculations or reasoning. To be excluded by the evaluating team as causes for the severe ability–achievement discrepancies were visual, hearing, or motor handicap, emotional disturbance, or environmental, cultural, or economic disadvantage. This definition of learning disabilities differs little from Kirk's original one in 1962 suggesting that the problems in identifying and classifying children with unexpected school difficulties are mainly operational rather than conceptual. However, children with learning problems have also been classified under other rubrics that include dyslexia, minimal brain dysfunction, and the hyperkinetic syndrome.

Dyslexia is a hardy but controversial diagnostic category (Eisenberg, 1978; Owen, Adams, Forrest, Stolz, & Fisher, 1971; Rutter, 1978). The term means reading disorder and its use implies an impairment of constitutional as opposed to environmental origin (Schain, 1977). Developmental dyslexia, as distinct from acquired dyslexia following brain injury, is assumed to be of genetic origin. Although reading scores are widely used as a criterion measure in studies of learning-handicapped children (Torgesen, 1975), this particular theoretical position is not usually implied.

In 1968, the World Federation of Neurology (Critchley, 1970) defined specific developmental dyslexia as "A disorder manifested by difficulty in learning to read despite conventional instruction, adequate intelligence and sociocultural opportunity. It is dependent upon fundamental cognitive disabilities which are frequently of constitutional origin" (p. 11). An influential supporter of this definition, Critchley had earlier defined dyslexia as a relatively rare congenital disorder of symbolic processes due to an immaturity of cerebral functions (Critchley, 1964). An opposite view of the World Federation of Neurology's definition of dyslexia was taken by Rutter (1978) who finds it logically unsatisfactory and practically unworkable. In his introduction to a collection of papers entitled "Dyslexia" (Benton & Pearl, 1978), Rutter concludes that the term does not refer to any well-defined group of disorders but rather is an important and plausible hypothesis that merits further investigation.

Minimal brain dysfunction (MBD) is a category that includes learning disabilities along with hyperactivity as symptoms of subclinical central nervous system damage. The most widely used definition is from Clement's report in 1966 of the findings of a task force on minimal brain dysfunction syndrome cosponsored by the National Institute of Neurological Diseases and Blindness. The term refers to:

> children of near-average, average or above average general intelligence with certain learning or behavioral disabilities ranging from mild to severe, which are associated with deviations of function of the central nervous system. These deviations may manifest themselves by various combinations of impairment in

> perception, conceptualization, language, memory, and control of attention, impulse or motor function. . . . These aberrations may rise from genetic variations, biochemical irregularities, perinatal brain insults or other illnesses or injuries sustained during the years which are critical for the development and maturation of the central nervous system, or from unknown causes . . . During the school years, a variety of learning disabilities is the most prominent manifestation of the condition. (p. 9, 10)

In a critical appraisal of this definition, Rie (1980) concludes that it is speculative and tentative and lacks an empirical base, but that it was not intended as a final statement on the consequences of presumed CNS impairment.

Definitions of MBD have been relatively consistent. They include learning and attentional difficulties, increased activity level, and minor perceptual and motor deficits attributed to dysfunction of the central nervous system (Gross & Wilson, 1974; Haller & Axelrod, 1975; Pincus & Glaser, 1966; Wender, 1973). The concept of MBD has its roots in studies of the sequelae of encephalitis and of known brain damage (Clements & Peters, 1962; Omenn, 1973; Orton, 1937; Strauss & Lehtinen, 1947). Children with behavioral abnormalities similar to those following documented CNS insult were assumed to have some underlying brain dysfunction, although minimal. More recently, Wender (1971) has proposed that the MBD syndrome results from an underlying abnormality in monoamine metabolism that is responsive to CNS stimulants and that affects both learning and activity level. The supportive evidence for this theory is at best suggestive (Cantwell, 1980; McMahon, 1981).

Cerebral dysfunction was included as an etiological factor in Kirk's original definition of learning disabilities but it has been dropped from most current definitions. In the 1980 *Diagnostic and Statistical Manual* of the American Psychiatric Association, behaviors formally subsumed under the labels of minimal brain dysfunction and hyperactivity are now categorized as attention deficit disorder (ADD). Learning disability is not considered to be a core symptom of ADD (Rapoport & Zametkin, 1980).

Hyperactivity or the hyperkinetic syndrome refers to excessive motor activity, distractability or inattention, and impulsivity. As a primary symptom of minimal brain dysfunction (Clements, 1966; Pincus & Glaser, 1966; Sulzbacher, 1975; Wender, 1973), hyperactivity shares the historical connection with childhood brain injury and is frequently associated with learning difficulties. Children who are classified as hyperactive are often assumed to be learning disabled (Delamater, Lahey, & Drake, 1981). In factor analytic studies, Safer and Allen (1976) and Lahey, Stempniak, Robinson, and Tyroler (1978) found hyperactivity and learning disabilities to be independent dimensions of problem behaviors. Investigations of hyperactivity are complicated by problems of definition and a lack of normative data (Barkley, 1981). Learning disabilities are more often objectively defined than hyperactivity where the only criterion may be a teacher or parent rating or a school or physician referral

(Berler & Romanczyk, 1980). Methodological issues aside, whereas excessive motor activity may interfere with learning, there seems to be little evidence that hyperactivity and learning disabilities have some more intrinsic association.

Most investigations of the causes of learning disabilities have focused on a single factor ranging in scope from lateral dominance to teaching techniques. Multivariate models have only recently been proposed in this complex area of research (Satz & Fletcher, 1980). Although the history of learning disabilities began with various etiological theories (Hallgren, 1950; Orton, 1937), there is little current agreement on causative factors or their relative importance. Some representative findings are reviewed from studies of family characteristics, genetic factors, perinatal complications, "maturational lag," and linguistic deficits.

Family Characteristics

In a recent review, Werner (1980) states that the most powerful environmental predictor of childhood learning and behavior disorders is the "social status and family characteristics of the caretaking environment" (p. 215). In addition to other studies, Werner cites evidence from her longitudinal investigation of the development of a cohort of children born on the island of Kauai. Reports from the Kauai study show that children from upper-middle class homes had high PMA IQ and reading, perceptual, and numerical factors scores at age 10 regardless of the presence of severe perinatal stress (Werner, Simonian, & Smith, 1967). Conversely, low socioeconomic status was associated with problems in language, perception, reading, and control of aggressive behavior. Of children in need of placement in a class for the learning disabled, three out of four were from low SES homes (Werner & Smith, 1977). Werner acknowledges that socioeconomic status is not a unitary concept and calls for more studies of process variables such as parent–child interactions.

Alberman (1973), drawing mainly on results from the English National Child Development Study, concludes that "overwhelmingly the best predictors of learning disability are poor socioeconomic circumstances, the child's position in the family, and the size of the family. Other predictors such as birthweight and abnormal neurological signs in infancy lag far behind" (p. 204). In a longitudinal study of academic performance of children from different social classes in Winnipeg, Bell and her colleagues found that lower socioeconomic status was associated with lower achievement test scores in reading and arithmetic even when IQ and a measure of school readiness were controlled (Bell, Abrahamson, & McRae, 1977; Bell, Aftanas, & Abrahamson, 1976). Other studies have found that both the educational level and marital status of the mother are related to childhood learning disorders (Kappelman, Rosenstein, & Ganter, 1972; Ramey, Stedman, Borders–Patterson, & Mengel, 1978).

In the longitudinal National Child Development Study referred to earlier, Davie, Butler, and Goldstein (1972) found a large effect of family size on reading scores and a smaller effect on arithmetic scores when social class and region (England, Scotland, or Wales) were controlled. The reading age of 7-year-olds from one or two child families was approximately 1 year ahead of those from families with five or more children. These investigators also found an independent effect of ordinal position in the family with firstborn reading about 16 months ahead of fourth or later born children. In another large population study, Belmont, Stein, and Wittes (1976) have shown that rates of educational failure increase with both increasing birth order and increasing family size in both manual and nonmanual social classes.

Sex of child, a characteristic often considered simultaneously with ordinal position in studies of family configuration, is strongly related to learning difficulties. The high incidence of boys among learning-disabled populations has been a consistent finding (Belmont, 1980; Critchley, 1964; Klasen, 1972). In a review of sex differences in abilities and behavior, Maccoby and Jacklin (1974) report that reading disabilities are from three to 10 times more common for boys depending on the definition of the disability and the sample studied. In a recent survey of 2000 children labeled and served as learning disabled in 22 states, the male to female ratio was almost four to one, a proportion in agreement with that found in a similar survey in 1972 (Norman & Zigmond, 1980). There is some evidence that girls considered in need of remedial education are more handicapped intellectually than are boys (Owen, 1978).

Genetic Studies

Genetic theories of learning disorders, or more precisely of reading disorders, date back to the beginning of this century when Hinshelwood and Morgan described congenital word blindness, and Thomas reported that this total or near-total inability to learn to read often occurred in more than one family member (Owen, 1978). Congenital word blindness was attributed by these early investigators to abnormalities in the angular and supramarginal gyri of the cerebral cortex. More recently, beginning with the work of Orton in 1930, many studies have reported a familial occurrence of language disorders and of "specific dyslexia" that suggests that these difficulties are inherited (Owen, 1978). Hallgren (1950) studied 116 children with specific dyslexia and found that 83% had parents with similar difficulties. He postulated that dyslexia probably followed a dominant mode of inheritance. Satz, Friel, and Goebel (1975) found a rate of familial occurrence of reading handicap similar to that found by Hallgren. Of 28 children with "pure" dyslexia, 80% had at least one parent with the disability whereas in a matched control group, 80% had parents without reading difficulties. Symmes and Rapoport's (1972) subjects with unexpected reading failure also had a high incidence of reading difficulties in their families. Siblings and parents of reading-disabled children were found to have similar deficits in an investigation by DeFries, Singer, Foch, and Lewitter (1978). Finucci and her associates (1976), examining immediate family members of a sample of 20 children with specific reading disability, found 45% of 75 first-degree relatives to be affected, primarily males. These investigators concluded that no single mode of genetic transmission was evident in the family pedigrees. A sample of disadvantaged learning-disabled children was found to have a greater frequency of sensory and behavioral difficulties in their family's histories than did their matched controls (Kappelman et al., 1972). Owen et al. (1971) reported similarities of impairment in siblings and mothers of a subgroup of educationally handicapped children with a high WISC performance IQ relative to verbal IQ. The sibling pairs were concordant for neurological and speech problems, and for WISC subscale patterns. The mothers of this subgroup had poor adult reading skills.

Twin studies have lent additional support to a genetic etiology for learning disorders. Both Hermann (1959) and Bakwin (1973) report a significantly higher degree of concordance for reading disabilities in monozygotic than in dizygotic twins. In her 1978 review, Owen concludes from her own and other findings that the marked familial incidence among some learning-handicapped groups is unequivocal. She proposes that multifactorial genetic predisposition is the source of at least one type of learning disability.

Evidence that learning disabilities can have a genetic basis has come from a prospective study of children identified as having sex chromosome anomalies at birth (Pennington, Bender, Puck, Salbenblatt, & Robinson, 1982). As compared with chromosomally normal siblings, the affected children were at increased risk for learning problems and special educational intervention. The learning disabilities that included a visuo–spatial deficit, a verbal language deficit, and a more global cognitive delay were karyotype specific, although there was considerable variability within a karyotype.

Perinatal Complications

The early view of learning disabilities as symptoms of brain damage and later of minimal brain dysfunction has resulted in studies of complications in pregnancy and the perinatal period as precursors of learning problems in children. As noted by Kessler (1980), Knobloch and Pasamanick were among the first to use the transitional term minimal cerebral damage to describe minor neurological and behavioral deviations in the newborn. Later retrospective studies by these investigators and their colleagues implicated pre and perinatal complications as causes of a variety of adverse outcomes and led to the hypothesis of a continuum of reproductive casualty with severe to minimal sequelae (Lilienfeld & Pasamanick, 1955).

The complications of low birthweight and of toxemia and bleeding in pregnancy were found to be associated with reading disorders in a retrospective study of white boys by Kawi and Pasamanick (1958, 1959). Versacci (1966) also found low birthweight, but only in combination with shortened gestation, to differentiate between high and low reading achievement in fifth grade children. Kappelman et al. (1972), comparing disadvantaged learning-disabled children and matched controls, found a greater incidence of maternal preeclampsia, breech delivery, and low birthweight in the learning-disabled group. Lyle (1970) reported that a group of symptoms of possible brain injury at birth predicted a measure of perceptual distortion but not of formal (verbal) learning difficulties. In this study, the best predictors of reading retardation were early speech difficulties. In two other retrospective studies, unusual birth histories (Galante, Flye, & Stephens, 1972) and neurological dysfunction in the newborn period (Francis–Williams, 1976) were found to be more frequent among retarded than among average readers. In two partially prospective studies in which the children to be followed were classified on the basis of retrospectively examined birth records, one or more complications of pregnancy or birth (Jordan, 1964) and prematurity (Caplan, Bibace, & Rabinovitch, 1963) were found to be associated with reading problems. In the latter study, the prematures had poorer reading skills than controls at ages 11 and 12 years but not at ages 7 and 8.

Among the results from longitudinal studies beginning at birth, Corah, Anthony, Painter, Stern, and Thurston (1965) failed to find a relationship between anoxia and oral reading ability at age 7 although the anoxic group had performed more poorly than controls on all tests of cognitive function at age 3. One subgroup of "postnatal" anoxics had low reading scores at the 7-year follow-up. In the British National Child Development Study, Davie et al. (1972) found significant independent effects of lower birthweight, heavy smoking in pregnancy, and maternal age under 25 on reading attainment at age 7. Among 22 learning-disabled 10-year-olds in the Kauai study, Werner and Smith (1977) found higher proportions of moderate perinatal stress, low birthweight, and congenital defects, but differences between this small group and their demographically matched controls were not statistically significant.

Rubin and Balow (1977), reporting on an extended follow-up to age 12 of a subsample of children in the Collaborative Perinatal Project, found significant but low correlations (.13 to .29) between sets of pregnancy and neonatal complications and school disabilities. From their own and other findings, these investigators concluded that socioenvironmental characteristics influence achievement and behavior in school much more strongly than any cluster of perinatal variables. Contrary to the British findings on maternal age, young mothers in the Collaborative Perinatal Project were not found to have an excess of low achieving children at age 7 when socioeconomic status was controlled (Broman, 1981). From a study of symptoms of minimal brain dysfunction in the Collaborative Perinatal Project, Nichols and Chen (1981) reported that only a very few of the 62 prenatal and perinatal characteristics examined were independently related to a learning difficulties factor score.

Maturational Lag

The theory that learning disorders are the result of developmental delay or lack of age-appropriate differentiation in a variety of response systems was proposed by Bender (1957). Maturational lag does not involve structural or functional defects and is characterized by Bender (1975) as "a less mature level of patterning in perceptual, mental, motor, and also visceral and autonomic behavior" (p. 435). The process of maturation is expected to continue in these children who, according to Bender, include the minimally brain damaged and schizophrenic as well as the learning disabled. An advocate of this theory, Kinsbourne (1973) states that "I have never seen a case of learning disability that was essentially any different from a younger child not yet ready to read" (p. 700). He suggests that damage to the developing nervous system from perinatal trauma or other insult results in a failure of the normal timing of development of the function subserved by the damaged area. Similarly, Satz has proposed that reading disorders reflect a lag in the maturation of the cerebral cortex that is expressed by delays in those skills that are most characteristic of a given chronological age—visual-perceptual skills in younger children and verbal ones in older children (Satz, Taylor, Friel, & Fletcher, 1978).

Studies of functional immaturity in learning-disabled children have focused on several basic processes including establishment of lateral dominance and lateral awareness, motor skills, visual and auditory perception, recall of verbal and nonverbal materials, and electrophysiological measures of cortical functioning. Right–left confusion but not any particular pattern of lateral dominance has been found to be associated with reading problems (Belmont & Birch, 1965; Benton, 1958, 1975; Crinella, Beck, & Robinson, 1971; Rosenberger, 1967; Rutter et al., 1970; Silver & Hagin, 1967). Naylor (1980) concluded from a review of experimental studies of lateral asymmetry in reading-disabled children that, due to the complexities of the tasks presented, poor performance could not be attributed to a hypothesized disorder of cerebral asymmetry. A symptom related to right–left disorientation is finger agnosia or difficulties with finger localization (Rourke, 1978). More localization errors have been reported among poor than normal readers, especially those who are age 10 or older (e.g., Finlayson & Reitan, 1976; Reed, 1967).

Minor motor disorders or clumsiness have often been associated with learning disorders, particularly among younger children (Ayres, 1972; Kephart, 1960; Peters, Romine, & Dykman, 1975). In an illustration of this approach, Peters et al. summarized the results of neurological examinations given to 82 learning-disabled boys between the ages of 8 and 11 years as follows: "These findings indicate that children with learning difficulties tend to have a delay in motor development and that improvement occurs first in gross motor functioning and body orientation. The developmental delay is assumed to be due to a delay in neurological maturation'' (p. 74). On the other hand, a review by Lucus (1980) of muscular control and coordination in minimal brain dysfunctions concludes that poor motor performance is neither an indicator of childhood brain damage nor a reliable predictor of learning problems primarily because of individual differences in rates of motor development through the elementary school years. Illingworth (1980) has also stressed the wide normal variation present in manual and motor dexterity. Freides, Barbati, van Kempen-Horowitz, Sprehn, Iverson, Silver and Woodward (1980), who found subtle but reliable deficits in motor reflexes as well as motor skills among learning-disabled boys, suggest that future research on motor factors is warranted despite their controversial role in learning disorders.

Perceptual problems in the visual, visual–motor, and auditory systems and in cross-modal integration have been cited as causes of learning difficulties, particularly in reading. Since Orton (1925, 1937) hypothesized that poor readers were developmentally delayed in their ability to recognize and reproduce visually presented symbols, and Bender (1956, 1957) suggested an underlying dysfunction in figure-ground organization, other investigators have associated learning disorders with perceptual–motor problems (Brenner, Gillman, Zangwill, & Farrell, 1967; Cruickshank, 1968; Cruickshank, Bentzen, Ratzberg, & Tannhauser, 1961; Frostig, 1972; Kephart, 1960). Johnson and Myklebust (1967) identified a group of visual dyslexics with problems that included perceiving the orientation of letters, and a group of auditory dyslexics with difficulties in recognizing and reproducing sounds. Others have reported that poor readers have deficits in the retention of auditory stimuli (Isom, 1968; Ring, 1976), and in the use of phonological cues (Bradley & Bryant, 1979). Birch (1962) identified a subgroup of poor readers with a delay in the ability to integrate information from different sense modalities, a process thought to influence at least the beginning stages of reading. Studies designed to test this hypothesis produced reliable differences between poor and normal readers on cross-modal matching tasks, but these differences could have been due to short-term memory factors or to difficulties within a given modality rather than in cross-modal transfer (Vellutino, 1978).

Memory may be a confounding factor in many tasks presented to learning-disabled children to investigate spatial disorientation or perceptual deficits. Poor recall is an etiological theory in its own right, particularly deficits in serial-order memory for verbal material (Bakker, 1972). Evidence for deficient rehearsal strategies among learning-disabled children on short-term memory tasks has been reported by Bauer (1977a, b) and Torgesen and Goldman (1977). Results obtained by Swanson (1979) suggest that recall difficulties in learning-disabled children are due to a deficiency in verbal mediation or the use of labels to mediate overt behavior. Short-term memory for verbal material is reported to be more susceptible to interference from verbal distractors among learning-disabled than among normal children (Cermak, Goldberg–Warter, DeLuca,

Cermak, & Drake, 1981). Reviewing research on memory skills and on selective attention, Torgesen (1980) concludes that the performance deficiencies of learning-disabled children, like those of normal younger children, are due primarily to inefficient task strategies rather than to limited capacity.

Immature or abnormal brain function as reflected in EEG patterns has been investigated as a cause of learning problems, particularly those in reading. A review by Hughes of electrophysiological studies with critiques by Denckla and Conners has been published in the proceedings of an NIMH conference on dyslexia (Benton & Pearl, 1978). Hughes concludes that although EEG findings in dyslexics and other learning-disabled children are controversial and beset by methodological problems, they are promising enough to warrant further study. The increased incidence of EEG abnormalities found among dyslexics includes positive spikes, occipital slow waves, and in some studies, diffuse abnormalities and epileptiform activity. In studies using other electrophysiological measures, the CNV or contingent negative variation, an "expectancy" waveform that follows a preparatory stimulus, has been found to be reduced in children with learning disorders, and visual and auditory evoked responses have been found to have lower amplitudes indicating decreased attentiveness. Denckla's critique (Benton & Pearl, 1978) emphasizes the methodological problems stemming from an inadequate definition of subjects, both dyslexic and normal, and is devoted mainly to the question "EEG correlates of *what?*" (p. 243). Conners cites many methodological flaws in the EEG studies that reduce the reliability of the findings and concludes that there is little empirical support for an association between EEG abnormalities and dyslexia per se, that is, when associated behavior or neurological abnormalities are excluded. He suggests, however, that evoked potential or CNV measures recorded during presentation of verbal stimuli may provide insight into the neurophysiology of reading disorders.

Linguistic Deficits

Studies reporting poor performance on linguistic tasks among learning-disabled children and adolescents have been reviewed by Bryan and Bryan (1980) and Vellutino (1978). Ludlow (1980) has reported that among preschool children with language impairments in expression and comprehension, 60% were in classes for the learning disabled at age 9. Kirk and Elkins (1975) found that of more than 3000 children receiving special education for learning disorders in 21 states, 24% were classified as having primary problems in language, as distinct from reading or spelling, and 43% were receiving remedial instruction in that area.

Early language difficulties have been categorized as a delay (Ludlow, 1980) and as a sign of maturational immaturity (Satz et al., 1978). Vellutino (1978) views the poor verbal skills of learning-disabled children as a specific, basic deficit that causes learning handicaps, primarily in reading. Based mainly on his own program of research on differential responses to verbal and nonverbal stimuli, Vellutino attributes the apparent perceptual and memory problems of poor readers to problems in verbal encoding including verbal mediation deficiencies and linguistic intrusion errors. No specific component of language (semantic, syntactic, or phonological) has been identified as most deficient among poor readers, nor have the origins of the linguistic deficits been described. One of the contributions of the verbal processing theory of reading disorders is the useful concept of maximum transfer. Both diagnostic tests and remedial techniques are designed to focus directly on the skill to be learned (Vellutino, Steger, Moyer, Harding, & Niles, 1977).

Other Etiological Factors

Among the other variables investigated as contributors to learning difficulties are complex ones such as the structure, climate, and value systems of schools (Goodman, 1964; Rutter, 1980), specific features of the English language and script (Makita, 1968), childhood emotional disturbances (Eisenberg, 1975; Rutter et al., 1970), and motivational factors (Yando, Seitz, & Zigler, 1979). Learning disabilities have also been related to malnutrition in early infancy (Klein, Forbes, & Nader, 1975), bottle as opposed to breast feeding (Rodgers, 1978), vestibular disorders and related postural disturbances (de Quiros, 1976), otitis media (Leviton, 1980; Masters & Marsh, 1978; Zinkus & Gottlieb, 1980), and prolonged or frequent hospitalization in early childhood (Douglas, 1975).

In summary, several themes are common to critiques of the large body of research on learning disabilities only a portion of which has been reviewed here. The central problem of definition, or as Benton (1978) says, "what the subject of investigation is" (p. 475) is reflected in many specific issues and procedures. Subjects are selected with nonuniform criteria and are often inadequately described with respect to characteristics that are highly related to school performance. Samples are frequently drawn from clinic or special class populations where multiple problems coexist with learning deficiencies in specific areas (Belmont & Birch, 1966; Symmes & Rapoport, 1972). Many studies are based on small samples, usually restricted to boys but often including a wide age range. Efforts to identify antecedents of learning disabilities have been mainly retrospective. Longitudinal data are needed to trace the development of learning problems and their relationship to various predictors over time. An important problem in interpretation is distinguishing between correlates and causes of unexpected learning difficulties. Many studies in this area are nonexperimental, although the trend is changing in reports published in education and psychology journals (Torgesen & Dice, 1980).

It is generally agreed that children classified as learning disabled are a heterogeneous group, and that a necessary first step in investigating antecedents, correlates, or methods of intervention is to select homogeneous subgroups (Fletcher, 1983). In the present study, the early development and abilities of a sample of low achieving children were compared with that of academically successful controls. Homogeneity was introduced by controlling for age and IQ score, analyzing potential predictors and correlates within ethnic and sex groups, and examining subgroups defined by extent of academic impairment, cognitive level, and behavior. Subjects were drawn from the population of 35,000 children followed from gestation to age 7 in the Collaborative Perinatal Project of the National Institute of Neurological and Communicative Disorders and Stroke.

The Collaborative Project was begun in 1959 to investigate the developmental consequences of complications in pregnancy and the perinatal period. Between that date and 1974, offspring from 53,000 pregnancies were followed from gestation through age 8 by multidisciplinary research teams in 12 medical centers. Women in the study were representative of the patients receiving prenatal care in the participating centers. Abnormal outcomes of special interest were cerebral palsy, mental retardation, congenital malformations, and learning disorders. Causes of prematurity and perinatal death and factors related to physical and cognitive growth were also investigated. The concept of a continuum of reproductive casualty, referred to earlier, was a major influence in the initiation and design of the Collaborative Project. There are several comprehensive reports describing the methodology and findings from this large-scale longitudinal investigation (Broman, 1984; Broman, Nichols, & Kennedy, 1975; Hardy, Drage, & Jackson, 1979; Lassman, Fisch, Vetter, & LaBenz, 1980; Niswander & Gordon, 1972). In a companion study to the present one, Nichols and Chen (1981) investigated the symptoms and antecedents of the minimal brain dysfunction syndrome in the Collaborative Project population.

In this study, low achievers are defined as children with IQ scores of at least 90 at age 7 and achievement levels in reading or spelling that were more than 1 year below grade placement, or for repeaters, no higher than grade placement. They were compared with IQ-matched controls on prenatal and perinatal characteristics and indices of physical and mental development through age 7. Because of the wide scope of the prospectively collected data, many of the etiological factors that have been associated with learning difficulties could be examined including family characteristics, prenatal and perinatal complications, neurological signs, and verbal and perceptual–motor abilities.

The main statistical procedure used was the multivariate technique of discriminant function analysis. For study and control groups, and for subgroups of study children, comparisons were made within and across developmental epochs and types of assessment.

2 Methods

The Sample and the Subgroups

The population of the Collaborative Perinatal Project was 53,043 women who registered for prenatal care in the 12 study centers (Table 1). At centers where all patients were not included during the 6 years of intake, a random selection was made (Broman et al., 1975). The sample for this study was drawn from a cohort of 34,875 white and black children followed to age 7. The cohort did not include children with unknown IQ, achievement test scores, or school grade or those who were 8 years or older at the time of the 7-year psychological examination.

The criteria for the selection of low achievers were a Full Scale IQ of 90 or above on the Wechsler Intelligence Scale for Children (Wechsler, 1949) and a grade rating on the reading or spelling subtest of the Wide Range Achievement Test (Jastak & Jastak, 1965) that was more than 1 year below grade placement, or for repeaters, no higher than grade placement. A sample of 994 children was identified. Among whites, the prevalence was 2.6% and among blacks, 3.1% (Table 2).[1] Of the 430 white low achievers, 121 had a low grade rating in reading, 153 in spelling, and 156 in both areas. Combining the first and third groups, the proportion of children with reading problems was 64%. Similarly, among the 564 black low achievers, 139 had a low grade rating in reading, 253 in spelling, and 172 in both areas. In this sample, 55% of the children were below grade placement in reading. The correlations between raw scores on the reading and spelling subtests were only .34 and .33 in the white and black

[1] If the cohort were restricted to children with IQs of 90 or above ($N = 23,939$), the prevalence would be 3.0% among whites and 5.8% among blacks.

Table 1
Sample Size by Institution and Ethnic Group in the Collaborative Perinatal Project Population

Institution	Ethnic Group				
	White	Black	Puerto Rican	Other	Total
Boston Lying-In Hospital	10,803	1,198	25	167	12,193
Providence Lying-In Hospital	2,096	672	5	49	2,822
Children's Hospital, Buffalo	2,383	59	12	15	2,469
Columbia-Presbyterian Medical Center	633	876	602	27	2,138
New York Medical College	269	1,558	2,630	17	4,474
Pennsylvania Hospital	882	8,580	316	14	9,792
Johns Hopkins Hospital	798	2,744	1	6	3,549
Medical College of Virginia	831	2,367	0	6	3,204
University of Tennessee College of Medicine	22	3,501	0	0	3,523
Charity Hospital, New Orleans	0	2,582	0	0	2,582
University of Minnesota Hospital	2,986	19	2	140	3,147
University of Oregon Medical School	2,216	861	1	72	3,150
Total	23,919	25,017	3,594	513	53,043

Table 2
Cohort and Study Group Frequencies

	Collab-orative Project Cohort	Low Achievers	Lower Achieving Subgroup	Hyper-active Subgroup	IQ Subgroups			Poorest Readers
					Low	Medium	High	
Whites								
Boys	8,598	297	111	63	116	126	55	32
Girls	8,163	133	45	17	68	56	9	12
Total	16,761	430	156	80	184	182	64	44
Blacks								
Boys	8,948	379	125	52	184	164	31	45
Girls	9,166	185	47	18	102	72	11	14
Total	18,114	564	172	70	286	236	42	59

samples of low achievers compared with values of .87 and .83 among the IQ-matched controls and .90 and .87 for all white and black children tested at age 7.

As shown in Table 2, 69% of white low achievers and 67% of black low achievers were male. Mean age in both samples was 85 ± 3 months.

Academically successful control subjects were selected for the low achievers in each ethnic group so that the IQ distributions in the study and control groups were identical. Control children had grade ratings on the reading, spelling, and arithmetic subtests of the WRAT that were at least equivalent to their grade placement. The control groups were six times as large as the low achiever groups (Table 3). Control group size was determined by the maximum number of controls available under the selection rule that the ratio of study to control children would be the same for each IQ value. Within this constraint, the controls were randomly selected. The mean age in both the white and black control groups was 84 ± 2 months.

Table 4 shows the criterion measures in the low achiever and control groups. Raw scores as well as grade ratings are reported for the reading and spelling subtests. Mean IQs were 98 and 96 in the white and black samples, respectively. Mean reading and spelling grade ratings were at the beginning first grade level for low achievers and were, of course, significantly lower than those in the control groups.

Other characteristics of low achievers and controls are shown in Tables 5 and 6. A lower Verbal than Performance IQ score for both groups in each sample is consistent with the scores of all children tested at age 7 in the Collaborative Project. Mean Verbal and Performance IQ scores were 101 ± 14 and 105 ± 16 for 17,000 white children and 89 ± 12 and 93 ± 14 for 19,000 black

Table 3
Control and Comparison Group Frequencies

	Low Achiever Controls	Lower Achieving Subgroup Controls	Hyperactive Comparison Group	Poorest Readers Controls
Whites				
Boys	1,276	1,469	233	32
Girls	1,304	1,495	116	14
Total	2,580	2,964	349	44
Blacks				
Boys	1,554	1,450	327	45
Girls	1,830	1,646	167	14
Total	3,384	3,096	494	59

Table 4
Means and Standard Deviations of WISC IQ Scores and WRAT Grade Ratings and Scores for Low Achievers and Controls

	Low Achievers	Controls	t	Low Achievers	Controls	t
	Whites					
	WISC Full Scale IQ					
Boys	98.38 ± 7.15	98.16 ± 7.22	0.47			
Girls	96.14 ± 6.01	97.23 ± 6.50	1.85			
Total	97.69 ± 6.89	97.69 ± 6.88	0.00			
	WRAT Reading Grade Rating			WRAT Reading Score		
Boys	1.22 ± 0.43	1.94 ± 0.83	14.39*	25.76 ± 6.66	35.96 ± 10.27	16.33*
Girls	1.22 ± 0.46	2.12 ± 0.84	12.00*	25.94 ± 6.76	38.42 ± 10.07	13.98*
Total	1.22 ± 0.44	2.03 ± 0.84	19.38*	25.81 ± 6.67	37.20 ± 10.24	22.28*
	WRAT Spelling Grade Rating			WRAT Spelling Score		
Boys	1.19 ± 0.27	1.77 ± 0.66	14.67*	19.91 ± 6.70	34.01 ± 7.95	17.68*
Girls	1.21 ± 0.25	1.96 ± 0.67	12.84*	20.10 ± 6.62	35.60 ± 8.08	12.66*
Total	1.20 ± 0.26	1.87 ± 0.67	20.30*	19.97 ± 6.71	34.87 ± 8.06	22.92*
	Blacks					
	WISC Full Scale IQ					
Boys	96.05 ± 5.51	95.91 ± 5.66	0.44			
Girls	95.27 ± 5.26	95.70 ± 5.23	1.05			
Total	95.79 ± 5.44	95.79 ± 5.44	0.00			
	WRAT Reading Grade Rating			WRAT Reading Score		
Boys	1.25 ± 0.44	1.77 ± 0.61	15.74*	26.19 ± 6.70	34.01 ± 7.95	17.68*
Girls	1.35 ± 0.42	1.88 ± 0.65	10.93*	27.83 ± 6.62	35.60 ± 8.08	12.66*
Total	1.28 ± 0.44	1.83 ± 0.63	19.87*	26.73 ± 6.71	34.87 ± 8.06	22.72*
	WRAT Spelling Grade Rating			WRAT Spelling Score		
Boys	1.16 ± 0.34	1.65 ± 0.52	17.25*	19.59 ± 3.14	23.94 ± 4.12	19.22*
Girls	1.22 ± 0.30	1.78 ± 0.56	13.51*	20.16 ± 2.89	24.97 ± 4.15	15.42*
Total	1.18 ± 0.32	1.72 ± 0.55	22.76*	19.78 ± 3.07	24.50 ± 4.17	25.76*

*$p < .00001$

Table 5
Verbal and Performance IQ Scores, Arithmetic Grade Rating and School Placement for Low Achievers and Controls in the White Sample

	Low Achievers			Controls			t or χ^2[1]
	N	Mean or Percent	SD	N	Mean or Percent	SD	
WISC Verbal IQ							
Boys	297	96.16	9.05	1,273	97.30	9.10	1.95
Girls	132	93.08	7.48	1,303	94.82	8.54	2.25*
Total	429	95.21	8.71	2,576	96.04	8.91	1.80
WISC Performance IQ							
Boys	297	101.15	10.21	1,274	99.42	9.99	2.67**
Girls	133	99.85	8.96	1,303	100.37	9.09	0.63
Total	430	100.75	9.85	2,577	99.90	9.55	1.69
WRAT arithmetic grade rating							
Boys	295	1.61	0.54	1,273	1.89	0.47	9.09***
Girls	133	1.59	0.48	1,301	1.96	0.43	9.41***
Total	428	1.60	0.52	2,574	1.93	0.45	13.49***
Repeating a grade							
Boys	297	56.57%		1,275	6.27%		<u>454.75</u>***
Girls	133	49.62%		1,304	4.14%		<u>320.31</u>***
Total	430	54.42%		2,579	5.20%		<u>827.30</u>***
Special class							
Boys	297	1.35%		1,274	1.02%		<u>0.03</u>
Girls	133	1.50%		1,304	0.77%		<u>0.15</u>
Total	430	1.40%		2,578	0.89%		<u>0.52</u>

[1]Chi-square statistic is underlined
* $p < .05$
** $p < .01$
***$p < .00001$

children. Low achievers had lower grade ratings on the Arithmetic subtest of the Wide Range Achievement Test than controls. More than one-half of low achievers in the white sample but less than one-fifth in the black sample were repeating a grade. Very few were enrolled in a special class. Grade placement for repeaters and nonrepeaters is described in a following section.

Five verbal and three performance subtests of the Wechsler Intelligence Scale for Children were administered at age 7. On the verbal subtests, low achievers in both samples had lower scores than their IQ-matched controls ($p < .05$) on Digit Span and Information, higher scores on Comprehension, and

Table 6
Verbal and Performance IQ Scores, Arithmetic Grade Rating and School Placement for Low Achievers and Controls in the Black Sample

	Low Achievers			Controls			t or χ^2
	N	Mean or Percent	SD	N	Mean or Percent	SD	
WISC Verbal IQ							
Boys	379	94.58	7.94	1,553	94.95	7.76	0.83
Girls	184	92.66	7.79	1,830	93.94	7.29	2.25*
Total	563	93.95	7.94	3,383	94.40	7.53	1.30
WISC Performance IQ							
Boys	379	98.12	8.92	1,553	97.64	8.94	0.94
Girls	184	99.07	8.41	1,830	98.33	8.22	1.16
Total	563	98.43	8.76	3,383	98.02	8.56	1.07
WRAT arithmetic grade rating							
Boys	379	1.57	0.53	1,553	1.85	0.50	9.48**
Girls	185	1.61	0.59	1,829	1.89	0.44	8.04**
Total	564	1.58	0.55	3,382	1.87	0.47	13.12**
Repeating a grade							
Boys	379	18.47%		1,554	1.29%		198.79**
Girls	185	16.76%		1,830	0.82%		184.22**
Total	564	17.91%		3,384	1.03%		408.76**
Special class							
Boys	379	0.79%		1,554	0.26%		1.16
Girls	185	1.08%		1,830	0.16%		2.61
Total	564	0.89%		3,384	0.21%		5.30*

* $p < .05$
**$p < .00001$

similar scores on Vocabulary. On the performance subtests, low achievers in the black sample had a lower score than controls on Picture Arrangement, those in both samples had higher scores on Coding and did not differ from controls on Block Design.

Four subgroups of low achievers were examined. The first was children who were more than 1 year below grade placement in both reading and spelling. This lower achieving subgroup, considered to be more academically impaired than the larger group from which it was drawn, represented less than 1% of the study cohort and about one-third of the low achievers in each sample (Table 2). Approximately 70% of the subgroup was male. Controls for the subgroup were selected from the same pool of cases as controls for the low achievers. Because there were fewer study subjects for a given IQ value, it was possible to select controls in ratios of 18 to 1 and 19 to 1 in the black and white samples, respectively (Table 3).

Criterion measures for the lower achieving subgroup are shown in Table 7. Mean IQs in the subgroup were essentially the same as those in the larger group. The proportion of repeaters was higher in the subgroup than the total group—76 versus 54% among whites and 28 versus 18% among blacks (Tables 8 and 9). In the latter sample, subgroup children, especially girls, were more frequently enrolled in a special class than those in the total group.

Grade in school for the low achievers and the lower achieving subgroup and their controls is shown in Table 10 tabulated separately for repeaters and nonrepeaters. A comparison with the criterion measures in Tables 4 and 7 shows that the mean difference between grade ratings and grade placement for study subjects was not always greater than 1 year. If expected rather than actual grade were used for repeaters, then the average grade placement for each group would be increased by an amount directly proportional to the percentage of repeaters in the group. For example, actual grade placement for white low achievers was 1.70, whereas grade placement would be 2.25 if expected rather than actual grade were used for repeaters in this group. This shows that the presence of repeaters had a marked effect on the difference between grade placement and WRAT grade ratings for the study groups. For white low achievers, this difference was $1.70 - 1.22 = .48$ for reading using actual grade placement for repeaters, and $2.25 - 1.22 = 1.03$ using expected grade placement for repeaters. The pattern of substantially larger differences between grade placement and grade ratings using expected rather than actual grade placement for repeaters was present for both the low achievers and the lower achieving subgroup, and for spelling as well as reading grade ratings. The grade placement–grade rating discrepancies that are less than 1 year are accounted for by the presence of repeaters.

A second subgroup of low achievers was those children with reading scores in the lowest 10% of the distribution. This subgroup of the poorest readers was selected without regard to grade placement and included 103 of the 994 low achievers (Table 2). The cutoff score of 17 was equivalent to a reading grade rating of Kindergarten .6. The mean reading score was 14.9 ± 2.1. The controls for the poorest readers were chosen from the control group for low achievers with one matched control selected for each of the 103 children in the subgroup. The control was chosen by matching exactly on WISC Full Scale IQ, prenatal socioeconomic index, age in months, sex, ethnic group, and institution of birth. The socioeconomic index, the major indicator of social class in this study, is an average of three scores for education and occupation of head of household and family income (Broman et al., 1975; Myrianthopoulos & French, 1968). When more than one child qualified as a control for a study

Table 7
Means and Standard Deviations of WISC IQ Scores and WRAT Grade Ratings and Scores for the Lower Achieving Subgroup and Controls

	Lower Achieving Subgroup	Controls	t	Lower Achieving Subgroup	Controls	t
Whites						
	WISC Full Scale IQ					
Boys	98.50 ± 7.26	98.04 ± 7.07	0.67			
Girls	95.96 ± 5.63	97.50 ± 6.70	1.53			
Total	97.77 ± 6.91	97.77 ± 6.89	0.00			
	WRAT Reading Grade Rating			WRAT Reading Score		
Boys	1.18 ± 0.31	1.91 ± 0.80	9.50*	24.94 ± 4.92	35.59 ± 10.13	10.99*
Girls	1.23 ± 0.34	2.13 ± 0.83	7.27*	26.04 ± 5.37	38.66 ± 9.97	8.46*
Total	1.19 ± 0.32	2.02 ± 0.82	12.48*	25.26 ± 5.06	37.14 ± 10.16	14.51*
	WRAT Spelling Grade Rating			WRAT Spelling Score		
Boys	1.21 ± 0.19	1.74 ± 0.61	9.19*	20.08 ± 1.88	24.54 ± 4.63	10.09*
Girls	1.24 ± 0.21	1.98 ± 0.67	7.40*	20.36 ± 2.10	26.38 ± 4.73	8.52*
Total	1.22 ± 0.19	1.86 ± 0.65	12.31*	20.16 ± 1.95	25.47 ± 4.77	13.84*
Blacks						
	WISC Full Scale IQ					
Boys	96.05 ± 5.80	95.62 ± 5.63	0.81			
Girls	94.36 ± 4.64	95.56 ± 5.44	1.49			
Total	95.59 ± 5.54	95.59 ± 5.54	0.00			
	WRAT Reading Grade Rating			WRAT Reading Score		
Boys	1.17 ± 0.36	1.74 ± 0.59	10.62*	24.92 ± 5.52	33.52 ± 7.76	12.13*
Girls	1.27 ± 0.35	1.87 ± 0.61	6.74*	26.74 ± 5.61	35.54 ± 7.86	7.62*
Total	1.20 ± 0.36	1.81 ± 0.60	13.18*	25.42 ± 5.59	34.59 ± 7.88	15.07*
	WRAT Spelling Grade Rating			WRAT Spelling Score		
Boys	1.18 ± 0.26	1.62 ± 0.51	9.68*	19.77 ± 2.62	23.68 ± 4.04	10.63*
Girls	1.28 ± 0.26	1.77 ± 0.55	6.08*	20.85 ± 2.60	24.90 ± 4.09	6.75*
Total	1.21 ± 0.26	1.70 ± 0.53	12.07*	20.06 ± 2.65	24.33 ± 4.11	13.45*

*$p < .00001$

Table 8
Verbal and Performance IQ Scores, Arithmetic Grade Rating and School Placement for the Lower Achieving Subgroup and Controls in the White Sample

	Lower Achieving Subgroup			Controls			t or χ^2[1]
	N	Mean or Percent	SD	N	Mean or Percent	SD	
WISC Verbal IQ							
Boys	111	96.20	8.98	1,468	97.08	8.76	1.02
Girls	45	92.51	6.41	1,494	95.00	8.72	1.90
Total	156	95.13	8.47	2,962	96.03	8.80	1.24
WISC Performance IQ							
Boys	111	101.43	9.62	1,468	99.45	9.80	2.06*
Girls	45	100.40	8.75	1,494	100.73	9.12	0.24
Total	156	101.13	9.36	2,962	100.09	9.48	1.34
WRAT arithmetic grade rating							
Boys	110	1.57	0.48	1,467	1.89	0.46	7.07****
Girls	45	1.69	0.49	1,493	1.97	0.45	4.19***
Total	155	1.61	0.49	2,960	1.93	0.45	8.71****
Repeating a grade							
Boys	111	77.48%		1,468	7.02%		<u>479.58</u>****
Girls	45	71.11%		1,495	3.81%		<u>351.10</u>****
Total	156	75.64%		2,963	5.40%		<u>891.98</u>****
Special class							
Boys	111	0.90%		1,467	1.43%		<u>0.00</u>
Girls	45	0.00%		1,495	0.80%		<u>0.07</u>
Total	156	0.64%		2,962	1.11%		<u>0.03</u>

[1]Chi-square statistic is underlined
* $p < .05$
** $p < .001$
*** $p < .0001$
**** $p < .00001$

subject, the selection was made randomly from all potential controls. The mean reading score for the 103 controls was 32.6 ± 6.3. Other characteristics of the poorest readers are reported in Chapter 6.

The third subgroup of low achievers received high ratings of four or five on a five-point level of activity scale at age 7. The hyperactive subgroups included 19% of white low achievers and 12% of black low achievers: The proportion of boys was 79 and 74%, respectively (Table 2). The hyperactive low achievers were compared with the remaining low achievers who were rated as average or below in activity level. This comparison group was therefore unlike the control

Table 9
Verbal and Performance IQ Scores, Arithmetic Grade Rating and School Placement for the Lower Achieving Subgroup and Controls in the Black Sample

	Lower Achieving Subgroup			Controls			t or χ^2
	N	Mean or Percent	SD	N	Mean or Percent	SD	
WISC Verbal IQ							
Boys	125	93.39	8.66	1,450	94.76	7.63	1.90
Girls	46	91.93	7.52	1,646	93.77	7.54	1.63
Total	171	93.00	8.37	3,096	94.23	7.59	2.06*
WISC Performance IQ							
Boys	125	99.12	8.94	1,450	97.26	9.01	2.22*
Girls	46	98.24	9.05	1,646	98.25	8.28	0.01
Total	171	98.88	8.95	3,096	97.79	8.64	1.61
WRAT arithmetic grade rating							
Boys	125	1.54	0.56	1,450	1.82	0.48	6.05****
Girls	47	1.61	0.60	1,646	1.89	0.43	4.33***
Total	172	1.56	0.56	3,096	1.86	0.46	8.14****
Repeating a grade							
Boys	125	31.20%		1,450	0.90%		321.58****
Girls	47	21.28%		1,646	0.97%		111.52****
Total	172	28.49%		3,096	0.94%		519.15****
Special class							
Boys	125	1.60%		1,450	0.28%		2.40
Girls	47	4.26%		1,646	0.18%		13.77**
Total	172	2.33%		3,096	0.23%		15.61***

* $p < .05$
** $p < .001$
*** $p < .0001$
**** $p < .00001$

groups previously described. The only differences between the hyperactive and nonhyperactive low achievers in IQ scores, grade ratings, or educational status were in the black sample where hyperactives had lower grade ratings in spelling ($p<.001$) and in arithmetic ($p<.05$) than nonhyperactives.

In the fourth of the subgroup analyses, low achievers with low (90–94), medium (95–104), and high (105–128) IQ scores were compared. Those with relatively high IQs were the subgroup of primary interest. The majority of low achievers (85% of the white sample and 93% of the black sample) had IQs

Table 10
Grade in School for Repeaters and Nonrepeaters: Low Achiever and Lower Achieving Study Groups and Controls

	Boys			Girls			Total		
	N	Mean	S.D.	N	Mean	S.D.	N	Mean	S.D.
White									
Low achiever group									
Repeaters	168	1.31	0.26	66	1.32	0.27	234	1.32	0.26
Nonrepeaters	129	2.15	0.41	67	2.18	0.39	196	2.16	0.41
Total	297	1.68	1.70	133	1.75	1.63	430	1.70	1.68
Low achiever controls									
Repeaters	80	1.15	0.29	54	1.21	0.26	134	1.18	0.28
Nonrepeaters	1,195	1.80	0.37	1,250	1.86	0.36	2,445	1.84	0.36
Total	1,275	1.77	0.57	1,304	1.84	0.54	2,579	1.81	0.57
Lower achieving subgroup									
Repeaters	86	1.38	0.22	32	1.45	0.24	118	1.40	0.23
Nonrepeaters	25	2.47	0.42	13	2.50	0.32	38	2.48	0.39
Total	111	1.62	2.25	45	1.75	2.20	156	1.66	2.23
Subgroup controls									
Repeaters	103	1.15	0.27	56	1.21	0.24	160	1.17	0.26
Nonrepeaters	1,365	1.80	0.36	1,438	1.86	0.35	2,803	1.83	0.36
Total	1,468	1.75	0.62	1,495	1.83	0.52	2,963	1.79	0.57
Black									
Low achiever group									
Repeaters	70	1.28	0.22	31	1.27	0.24	111	1.28	0.23
Nonrepeaters	309	2.25	0.38	154	2.33	0.37	463	2.28	0.38
Total	379	2.07	1.10	185	2.15	1.09	574	2.09	1.14
Low achiever controls									
Repeaters	20	1.10	0.16	15	1.21	0.25	35	1.15	0.20
Nonrepeaters	1,534	1.91	0.33	1,815	1.93	0.33	3,349	1.92	0.33
Total	1,554	1.90	0.40	1,830	1.92	0.38	3,384	1.91	0.39
Lower achieving subgroup									
Repeaters	39	1.36	0.22	10	1.33	0.24	49	1.35	0.22
Nonrepeaters	86	2.49	0.41	37	2.62	0.29	123	2.53	0.38
Total	125	2.13	1.53	47	2.34	1.36	172	2.17	1.50
Subgroup controls									
Repeaters	13	1.14	0.17	16	1.26	0.26	29	1.29	0.23
Nonrepeaters	1,437	1.90	0.33	1,630	1.93	0.33	3,067	1.91	0.33
Total	1,450	1.89	0.38	1,646	1.92	0.39	3,096	1.90	0.38

below 105 and, as shown in Table 2, were approximately equally distributed between the low and medium IQ groups. Grade ratings in reading, spelling, and arithmetic increased linearly across IQ subgroups in both samples ($F>8.20$, $p<.001$). School placement did not differ among the IQ subgroups.

Procedures

Study and control/comparison groups were compared on 391 characteristics derived from examinations and interviews conducted in the Collaborative Perinatal Project (Appendices 2 and 3). The data were recorded on standardized precoded protocols and, when completed, sent to the Perinatal Research Branch at the NINCDS for editing and transfer to computer tape, with copies retained by the collaborating institutions at each site. Instruction manuals accompanied each protocol, and workshops and training sessions were held periodically for research personnel. The major points of data collection were during prenatal visits, at delivery and in the newborn nursery, during infancy and the preschool period, and at age 7. A summary of the protocols is presented in Table 11.

During visits to the prenatal clinic, the mother provided interviewers with her medical history, socioeconomic and genetic information about herself and her family, and the baby's father and his family. Obstetricians recorded the results of physical examinations, histories, and laboratory tests. Prenatal clinic visits were scheduled every month during the first 7 months of pregnancy, every 2 weeks during the eighth month, and every week thereafter. At admission for delivery, the mother's physical status was reevaluated, and the events of labor and delivery were recorded by a trained observer. A summary of labor and delivery was completed by the obstetrician in charge. The placenta was examined by pathologists who also conducted postmortem examinations of stillbirths and neonatal deaths.

The neonate was observed initially in the delivery room and examined by a pediatrician at 24-hour intervals in the newborn nursery. A neurological examination was performed at 2 days of age. Other information from the nursery period included nurses' observations and the results of laboratory tests. A diagnostic summary of the nursery period was completed by a physician on the research team.

After the neonatal stage, the child was seen at specified intervals. At each follow-up examination, the mother was interviewed about the child's interval history, with records of medical treatment obtained if indicated, and the child's physical measurements were taken. A pediatric examination was given at 4 months, psychological examinations at 8 months, and 4 and 7 years, pediatric-neurological examinations at 1 and 7 years, and speech, language, and hearing examinations at 3 and 8 years. Interval histories were kept up to date at 18 months, and at 2, 5, and 6 years. Family and social history information was

Table 11
Summary of Protocols of the Collaborative Perinatal Project

Prenatal	
Registration and First Prenatal Visit	Subsequent Prenatal Visits
Obstetric administrative record Reproductive and gynecological history and history since last menstrual period Recent and past medical history including infectious disease and system review Socioeconomic interview Family history interview including outcomes of prior pregnancies, family composition and health history of parents and their relatives	Repeat prenatal history Prenatal observations Laboratory record Physician's clinic record Blood samples for serological studies Summary of antepartum hospitalization
Labor and Delivery	
Repeat prenatal history and admission history Admission examination Laboratory record Labor room record Delivery room events Delivery report	Obstetric summary Anesthetic agents Summary of puerperium Placental examinations (gross and microscopic) Obstetric diagnostic summary
Newborn	
Delivery room observation Neonatal examination Nursery history	Results of tests and procedures Neonatal neurological examination Newborn diagnostic summary
Four Months	
Pediatric examination	Interval medical history[a]

(continued)

Table 11 (Continued)

Eight Months	
Bayley Scales of Mental and Motor Development Infant behavior profile, maternal behavior ratings, and additional observations	Physical measurements Interval medical history
12 Months	
Neurological examination Interval medical history	Diagnostic summary of the first year
18 and 24 Months	
Interval medical history	
Three Years[b]	
Speech, language and hearing examination with tests of language reception and expression, auditory memory and discrimination, speech mechanism and production, and additional observations	Physical measurements Interval medical history
Four Years	
Stanford-Binet Intelligence Scale Graham-Ernhart Block Sort Test Gross and fine motor tasks Behavior profile and additional observations Science Research Associates (SRA) nonverbal intelligence test administered to mother	Physical measurements Interval medical history
Five and Six Years	
Interval medical history	

(continued)

Table 11 (Continued)

Seven Years	
Wechsler Intelligence Scale for Children	Pediatric neurological examination
Goodenough Harris Draw-A-Person Test	Visual screening and ophthalmology report
Bender-Gestalt Test	Interval medical history
Auditory-Vocal Association Test (Illinois Test of Psycholinguistic Abilities)	Diagnostic summary for years one through seven
Tactile Finger Recognition Test (Halstead-Reitan Battery)	
Wide Range Achievement Test	
Behavior profile and additional observations	
Family health history and socioeconomic interview with mother	
Eight Years[c]	
Speech, language and hearing examination with tests of language comprehension and expression, auditory discrimination, speech mechanism and production, and additional observations	Physical measurements Interval medical history
General Forms	
Administrative reports for record inventory, patient follow-up and sample maintenance	Report of fetal, infant, or child death Autopsy report

[a] All interval medical histories included summaries of medical records of illness.
[b] Examinations not administered at Children's Medical Center in Boston or Philadelphia Children's Hospital.
[c] Examinations administered only at the following six institutions: Buffalo Children's Hospital, Children's Medical Center in Boston, Johns Hopkins University, University of Tennessee, University of Minnesota, and University of Oregon.

obtained from the mother at the time of the 7-year examinations. Diagnostic summaries were prepared by physicians following the first year and the seventh year.

Data collection in the Collaborative Project covered a span of 16 years beginning in 1959 and ending in 1974. Not all subjects were given each examination. Problems of maintaining adequate follow-up are typical ones in longitudinal studies, and the large-scale Collaborative Project was no exception. The number and characteristics of children lost to the study have been discussed in detail elsewhere (Broman et al., 1975; Hardy et al., 1979; Niswander & Gordon, 1972). Follow-up rates for survivors in the total population of 53,042 pregnancies were 88% at 1 year, 75% at 4 years, and 79% at 7 years. At 3 and at 8 years, speech, language and hearing examinations were not given at all institutions (as noted in Table 11), and follow-up rates were only 48 and 47%, respectively. The missing data analyses discussed in a following section indicate that the absence of complete information on these factors was not likely to have influenced the major findings of the study.

Variables that were significant discriminators between or among the low achievers and control/comparison groups are defined when required in the chapters describing results. Information obtained from the maternal and child assessments was categorized into five epochs: early prenatal demographic; pregnancy and perinatal; infancy; preschool; and age 7. Classification of variables into these epochs permitted analyses of factors associated with low achievement within the five time periods separately and then across the epochs taken together. Precursors of low achievement were identified from each of the first four epochs and primarily correlates from the fifth epoch although some historical information was collected at this time. Because of the number and range of factors assessed in the fifth epoch, variables were further subdivided into three types. The general information contained in each epoch is summarized in the following sections.

1. Family and Maternal Characteristics. Of 26 demographic, family, and maternal variables screened, 25 were obtained from interviews with the mother in the prenatal period including age, parity, and education of the mother, socioeconomic status and composition of the family, and conditions in family members such as mental retardation or mental illness. Maternal score on the SRA nonverbal intelligence test was included in this epoch.

2. Pregnancy and Perinatal Conditions. The 114 variables screened consisted of complications and other characteristics of pregnancy such as weight gain and amount of prenatal care, events during labor and delivery including length of labor, fetal heart rate, and type of delivery, and indices of neonatal status such as gestational age, birthweight, Apgar score, respiratory events, and serum bilirubin level.

3. Characteristics During Infancy. Measures of physical and cognitive development during the first year of life included height, weight, and head circumference at 4 and at 12 months, a research version of the Bayley Scales of Infant Development at 8 months, and a pediatric examination at 1 year of age. Forty-three variables were screened.

4. Preschool Characteristics. Data from the preschool epoch consisted of four summary ratings from the speech, language, and hearing examination at age 3, and results from the 4-year psychological examination that included an assessment of intellectual functioning (Stanford–Binet Intelligence Scale), motor skills, concept formation ability (Graham–Ernhart Block Sort Test), and behavior in the testing situation. Three physical measurements obtained at age 4 were also screened resulting in a total of 39 preschool variables.

5. Characteristics at Age 7:

1. Demographic, family, and maternal characteristics were reassessed at the time of the 7-year examinations in an interview with the mother or other caretaker. Twenty-five variables were screened.
2. Medical status and medical history were evaluated in 120 variables drawn from a pediatric-neurological examination and a summary of interval medical histories taken between ages 1 and 7 years.
3. Intellectual and perceptual–motor functioning was assessed by a battery of instruments that included the Wechsler Intelligence Scale for Children,[2] the Goodenough Harris Draw-a-Person Test, the Bender–Gestalt Test, the Auditory Vocal Association Test from the Illinois Test of Psycholinguistic Abilities, and the Tactile Finger Recognition Test. Academic achievement was evaluated with the Wide Range Achievement Test, and ratings were made of behaviors observed in the testing situation. Twenty-four variables were screened.

Analytic Approach

Ethnic Group and Sex Differences. With one exception, all analyses were performed separately for blacks and whites. This approach was taken to avoid any confounding from ethnic group differences in level of cognitive performance (Yando et al., 1979), and from possible differences in predictors of achievement, similar to those found for IQ (Broman et al., 1975). Sex of child was initially treated as a potential discriminator or independent variable in the same manner as all other variables. Thereafter, for the low achievers and the lower achieving subgroup, where the sample of girls was sufficiently large, separate analyses were conducted by sex within each ethnic group. Girls are consistently underrepresented in samples of learning-disabled children, suggesting that etiological factors may differ in the two sexes.

Basic Analysis Sequence. Similar procedures were followed in performing the statistical analyses for low achievers, the lower achieving subgroup, the hyperactive subgroup, and the subgroup of poorest readers. With the exception of the subgroup of poorest readers where ethnicity as well as sex was a variable used in selecting matched controls, the basic procedures were carried out in each ethnic group separately and consisted of:

---

[2] The Arithmetic, Similarities, Object Assembly, and Picture Completion subtests were omitted.

1. Univariate Tests: Each of the 391 variables was analyzed to determine if the mean value differed significantly between the study group (subgroup) and control (comparison) group. *T*-tests and χ^2-tests were used for this purpose and differences were considered significant at $p<.05$.

2. Two-Group Discriminant Function Analyses: Stepwise two-group discriminant function analyses were then conducted using the variables for which significant mean differences were found in the univariate tests. The variables that were statistically significant ($p<.05$) in the discriminant function analyses are called discriminators between the appropriate study group (subgroup) and the control (comparison) group. The tables presented in subsequent chapters contain the results of the univariate and discriminant function analyses for the discriminators, i.e., only those variables that were significant in the discriminant function analyses. This approach may exclude certain variables that passed the univariate screen from becoming discriminators because of the correlation structure among potential discriminators. To avoid overlooking possible important results due to this problem, variables passing the univariate screen but not retained as discriminators were reviewed for presentation if judged appropriate.

3. Within-Epoch Analyses: The preceding two steps were conducted separately within each of the first four epochs and each of the three groups of variables in the fifth epoch. Appendix 2 contains a chart of all variables that passed the univariate screen by epoch and indicates the comparisons, if any, in which each variable was a discriminator.

4. Across-Epoch Analyses: Upon completion of the within-epoch analyses, the discriminators from the first four epochs were analyzed using stepwise discriminant function analyses. The intent was to determine the variables that would remain as significant discriminators when pooled with important factors from other epochs. Similarly, the significant discriminators from the three groups of variables in Epoch 5 were pooled. Thereafter, a final stepwise discriminant function analysis was conducted using the significant discriminators from the pooled analyses for Epochs 1 through 4 and for the three categories from Epoch 5. The rationale in pooling all epochs was to assess the magnitude or extent of the explanatory power of all independent precursors and correlates of low achievement combined. In the following chapters, results of the three across-epochs analyses from gestation through age 4, at age 7, and throughout the time span are presented. Many of the within-epoch findings not retained in the pooled analyses are also reported.

IQ Subgroup Analysis Sequence. The statistical procedures used in the IQ subgroup analyses differed slightly from those given previously. Because these analyses involved comparisons among three groups, analysis of variance, a different χ^2-procedure, and three-group discriminant function analysis were used instead of the aforementioned *t*-test, χ^2-test, and two-group discriminant function procedures. Aside from these differences, the separate analyses by ethnic group and epoch, as well as the pooled analyses across epochs, were the same as those in the basic analysis sequence.

Institutional Differences. In order to assess the effects of differences among study centers on the final results, univariate tests were conducted to determine if the percentage of children in each group (subgroup) and control (comparison) group differed by institution, using chi-square tests at the 5% significance level. These data are shown for low achievers in Table 1 of Appendix 4. The poorest readers and controls were matched on institution and therefore not included in this analysis. When significant study center differences were found between study and control (comparison) groups, the appropriate institutional indicators were included in the final across-epoch discriminant function analyses to determine whether controlling for these differences would alter the relative importance of other variables in the discriminant function. The results of these institutional analyses are reported in the respective chapters and tabulated in Appendix 4.

Statistical Methods

Analysis Orientation. Given the large number of potential relationships examined in this study, statistical techniques were selected using two criteria. First, it was required that the techniques be appropriate in that they yield information and results relevant to the major questions under investigation. This criterion required techniques that would not only give reasonably accurate significance levels, but also techniques accompanied by meaningful statistics that reflect the actual strength of associations in addition to significance. The second criterion required that the statistical procedures be reasonably well known and accepted for application to the data that had been collected, especially in the context of departures from underlying theoretical assumptions associated with the procedures. The rationale for the second criterion was based on the magnitude and complexity of the many relationships that this study addressed.

Because it was not possible to ensure that every theoretical assumption required by the statistical techniques was satisfied, departures from certain assumptions were investigated and appropriate qualifications are presented in the next section. Further, owing to the magnitude of the study, no pretense is made that each individual relationship between low achievement and a potential precursor or correlate was investigated using the (unequivocally) optimal technique. In this sense, the study is data analytic in nature and relies on the robustness of the techniques employed.[3]

Two-Group t and χ^2 Tests. In comparing differences in means between study and control groups, standard χ^2 and *t*-tests were used for dichotomous and continuous variables, respectively. The chi-square procedure is designed to test the equality of two proportions. The Yates continuity correction was used that, according to some authors, is a conservative approach to statistical testing (Grizzle, 1967; Plackett, 1964).[4] The *t*-test was the standard one for mean differences and is based on the assumption of equal variances (Mendenhall & Ott, 1980). A discussion of this assumption appears in the next section.

Two-Group Discriminant Function Analysis. To determine which variables discriminated between study and control groups in a multivariate context, a stepwise two-group discriminant function procedure was used. Variables were entered into or deleted from the discriminant function at the .05 level of significance.

Three-Group F and χ^2 Tests. For the IQ subgroup analyses, the two-group *t*-test and χ^2-test were extended to a one-way analysis of variance or *F*-test comparing three means and a χ^2-test for three proportions. The three-group analysis of variance procedure is a generalization of the two-sample *t*-test for equal means. The χ^2-test for the equality of three proportions was used for comparing dichotomous variables across the three IQ groups (Randles & Wolfe, 1979). After conducting the three-group *F*-or χ^2-tests, and the three-group discriminant function procedure summarized next, two-group *t*-tests and χ^2 tests were also conducted between pairs of IQ subgroups for variables that were significant in the three-group discriminant function analysis. Results of the two-group tests, not the three-group tests, are presented in Chapter 8 with the discriminant function results.

Three-Group Discriminant Function Analysis. A stepwise three-group discriminant function procedure was used to assess whether variables whose means or proportions differed significantly among the three IQ groups were also significant in the context of other variables. The three-group discriminant

---

[3] The phrase "data analytic" refers to studies or methods associated with exploratory data analysis and techniques that are not overly sensitive to departures from the theoretical assumptions on which they are based. The term *robustness* is a statistical term used to gauge the insensitivity of a statistical test or procedure to departures from its underlying assumptions (Mosteller & Tukey, 1977).

[4] The large sample sizes in this study very likely make the continuity correction issue inconsequential.

function procedure was similar to the two-group procedure in terms of stepwise entry of variables and the significance levels adopted. The three-group approach yielded two separate discriminant functions, with the first having optimal discriminatory power and the second having optimal discriminatory power among the class of linear discriminant functions that are orthogonal to (uncorrelated with) the first function. The same variables appear in both functions and the discriminatory power of the first is always greater than that of the second. Only the coefficients for the first function are presented in Chapter 8.

Statistics Associated With Discriminant Function Analyses. A brief explanation of and references for three terms associated with discriminant function analysis are appropriate because of their consistent appearance in tables presented in subsequent chapters.

1. Coefficients. Discriminant function coefficients can be standardized or unstandardized (Timm, 1975).[5] Standardized coefficients were used in presenting the findings of this study because they are not dependent on the original scale of the variables and often range between -1 and $+1$. The magnitude of the standardized coefficient represents a specific variable's contribution to the calculation of a discriminant score that can be used to classify individual cases. It reflects the contribution of the variable to the discriminatory strength of the function in a multivariate context. A negative sign accompanying a coefficient indicates that the mean value or frequency of the variable is lower in the study group than in the control/comparison group.

Except when a stepwise procedure is employed, no straightforward indicator of the statistical significance of a given coefficient is possible. An advantage of the stepwise procedure is its ability to assess whether a variable makes a statistically significant contribution to the overall discriminatory power of the linear discriminant function. However, as with any stepwise procedure, specific variables may fail to enter because of their association with variables that entered the discriminant function on preceding steps. This was monitored by comparing the discriminant function results with the univariate tests.

---

[5] When unstandardized coefficients are used in discriminant analysis, a constant term is also regarded as one of the coefficients (akin to regression analysis). This raises the issue of prior probabilities, i.e., whether they should be equal or given by the relative proportions of the sample sizes for two groups. Equal prior probabilities were used in this study because the ratio of controls to study subjects did not reflect the true ratio in the population, and, more importantly in either event, the prior probabilities do not influence coefficients other than the constant term (of the classification functions). Also, the classification probabilities, discussed later in 3, are slightly more conservative because the use of relative proportions would have increased the percentages of correct classifications and lowered the percentages of misclassifications.

2. Canonical Correlations. The fundamental intent of two-group discriminant function analysis is to construct a linear function that has mean values for group 1 and group 2 such that the difference between these two mean values is as large as possible. Several statistics are available to measure this distance or the general strength of the discriminant function (Goldstein & Dillon, 1978). One such statistic is an analog of the R, or multiple correlation (coefficient of determination), in regression analysis, a widely used method of data analysis (Klecka, 1979). The canonical correlation associated with the two-group discriminant function analysis has the same basic meaning as the R in regression analysis; that is, the square of the canonical correlation can be interpreted as the percentage of variation in the dichotomous (group indicator) variable due to or associated with variation in the discriminators. The probability value associated with the χ^2-test for overall significance of the discriminant function can be interpreted in a manner analogous to the probability value associated with the F-statistic for R in regression analysis. The canonical correlation for each discriminant function in a three-group analysis has a similar interpretation.

3. Classification Matrix. Once a discriminant function has been estimated, it can be used to classify observations into groups. In the case of two-group analysis, the matrix of frequencies or percentages that indicates whether the discriminant function classified each group 1 or group 2 observation correctly or incorrectly is termed the classification matrix (Klecka, 1979). This matrix is constructed so that the number or percentage of correctly classified cases is contained in the diagonal elements. Thus, the larger the frequencies and proportions on the diagonal of this matrix, the greater the discriminatory power. To conserve space, the percentage of correctly classified cases are presented in the tables that follow.

Statistical Assumptions

Although the statistical methods used are appropriate from the perspective of the two criteria given at the outset, a brief discussion of violations of underlying assumptions and the expected effects of such violations is warranted.

1. Normality. Both the *t*-test and *F*-test for analysis of variance assume that the variable of interest has an underlying normal distribution. These tests are generally regarded as robust relative to deviations from normality (Bradley, 1968). Nevertheless, for variables with distributions characterized by very few distinct values, or distributions that might be highly asymmetric or skewed, significance levels associated with these two tests should be regarded as approximate.[6] Chi-square tests were used for dichotomous variables, thereby avoiding this problem for variables that take on but two values.

[6] Because the distribution of the sample mean approximates a normal distribution as sample sizes increase, the normality assumption is not likely to be problematic for this study.

Most polytomous variables examined in this study took on a number of values or had distributions that were not severely skewed. However, Appendix 1 contains descriptive statistics, including a skewness indicator, for all variables that passed the univariate screen for low achievers so that they can be evaluated from other perspectives on departures from normality.

In discriminant function analysis, the vector of discriminators is assumed to follow a multivariate normal distribution. Linear discriminant function techniques are, however, also regarded as relatively robust with respect to deviations from this assumption (Goldstein & Dillon, 1978; Knoke, 1982). Further, the intuitive interpretation of the canonical correlation remains intact regardless of the underlying multivariate distribution that characterizes the vector of discriminators. Many of the discriminant function results presented in the following chapters are based on functions that involve both continuous and dichotomous variables. Discriminant analysis was selected as the fundamental multivariate technique rather than logistic regression or certain other classification procedures because it could be used in a stepwise manner, and because of the utility of the canonical correlation in characterizing the discriminatory power of variables within epochs and pooled chronologically across epochs. It is to be emphasized, however, that the discriminant function procedure was used as a data analytic tool and the significance level associated with the χ^2-test for the explanatory power of the discriminant function is approximate.

2. *Equality of Variances and Covariance Matrix Equality.* Both the univariate t-tests and F-tests for analysis of variance assume the variable under consideration has equal variances in the two (or three) groups under consideration. Both tests are known to be less robust relative to deviations from the equal variance assumption (Bradley, 1968). To assess the extent to which violations of this assumption would alter results, 20 variables were randomly selected for further analysis. Ten of the variables were significant and 10 were insignificant using the equal variance t-test for differences in low achiever and control means. Nineteen of the 20 did not change categories (i.e., from significant to insignificant or vice versa) when the unequal variance t-test was used. The one that did change categories was significant ($p = .043$) using the pooled variance test and insignificant ($p = .057$) using the separate or unequal variance. The observed tendency for the pooled variance test to yield lower p-values may have resulted in a small number of variables passing the univariate screen that would not have passed if the separate variance test were used. The data presented in Appendix 1, however, allow for the use of independent criteria (other than those used here) in judging the extent of group differences in variances.

Extending the concept of variance equality to the multivariate case, the two- and three-group discriminant function procedures employed assume equality of covariance matrices for the vectors of discriminators across the separate groups. In general, the assumption of covariance matrix equality was not tested, but the univariate assessments comparing the results of the pooled and separate variance t-tests suggest that violations of this assumption, although resulting in approximate p-values, would be unlikely to alter the major study findings.

3. Missing Data. As is evident from Appendix 1, most variables did not have complete values for all cases. For the most part this was not a major issue, but some variables had a high frequency of missing values. If only cases with complete data had been analyzed in this study, the actual number of cases would be extremely low because of the large number of variables examined. Further, if each discriminant function analysis had been conducted using only data with complete cases, then nearly all discriminant functions would be estimated using different (but overlapping) samples of cases. For these reasons, discriminant function analyses were conducted using correlation (covariance) matrices computed on the basis of pair-wise complete information (case by case) for all variables of interest.

To investigate the ramifications of this approach to treating incomplete data, two procedures were carried out on a representative set of discriminant function analyses tabulated in subsequent chapters. First, for each discriminant function chosen, the variable with the highest proportion of incomplete values was selected and a second discriminant function, using the same discriminators as the first, was estimated using only cases with complete data on that variable. Discriminant function coefficients and canonical correlations were then compared from the original discriminant function and the "complete cases" discriminant function. Second, cases with complete data for the variable with the most missing values were regarded as belonging to group 1 and cases with incomplete values for that variable were assigned to group 2. A discriminant function analysis was then conducted using the remaining discriminators in the original function to test for a pattern of association between complete and incomplete cases in terms of the remaining discriminators. The results of the first type of missing data analysis for several discriminant functions are illustrated in Table 12.

The discriminant function analyses shown in Table 12 were deliberately selected to include discriminators with unusually large amounts of incomplete information. Appendix 1 indicates the extent of data missing for all variables that passed the univariate screen in the basic comparison between low achievers and controls. The results of the second type of missing data analysis are not presented because the canonical correlations were small, always less than the canonical correlation for the original discriminant function, and often insignificant. On the basis of several analyses such as those summarized in Table 12, it did not appear that the approach to handling incomplete cases had any major effect on the overall findings of the study.

Because the χ^2 statistic for the significance of the discriminant function involves the sample size in its calculation, the question of how to compute the sample size arises in the presence of missing data. Alternatives include the

Table 12
Results of Discriminant Function Analyses to Examine Study Approach to Handling Incomplete Data

Example 1 Preschool discriminators between low achievers and controls for whites: Incomplete data for 46% of the low achievers and 53% of the control cases for abnormal speech production in original analyses.

	Original Discriminant Function (Chapter 3)	Discriminant Function Using Only Complete Cases for Variable 3
Study N	430	234
Control N	2,580	1,211
Canonical correlation	.18	.17
Standardized coefficients		
1. Stanford-Binet IQ	−.87	−.88
2. Activity level rating	.29	.18
3. Abnormal speech production (3 yrs.)	.26	.33

Example 2 Preschool discriminators between low achievers and controls for blacks: Incomplete data for 47% of the low achievers and 46% of the control cases for abnormal language expression in original analyses.

	Original Discriminant Function (Chapter 3)	Discriminant Function Using Only Complete Cases for Variable 2
Study N	564	299
Control N	3,384	1,819
Canonical correlation	.15	.15
Standardized coefficients		
1. Stanford-Binet IQ	−.45	−.47
2. Abnormal language expression (3 yrs.)	.39	.35
3. Head circumference	−.36	−.40
4. Graham Block Sort score	−.36	−.37
5. Dependency rating	.27	.22

(continued)

Table 12 (Continued)

Example 3 Early discriminators between hyperactive and non-hyperactive low achievers for blacks: Incomplete data for 33% of the hyperactive and 45% of the non-hyperactive cases for hydramnios in original analyses.

	Original Discriminant Function (Chapter 7)	Discriminant Function Using Only Complete Cases for Variable 2
Study N	70	47
Control N	494	273
Canonical correlation	.29	.30
Standardized coefficients		
1. Activity level rating	.61	.55
2. Hydramnios at delivery	.69	.67
3. Inhalation anesthetics at delivery	.40	.51

Example 4 Early discriminators between low achievers and controls for whites: Incomplete data for 16% of the low achievers and 16% of the control cases for Stanford-Binet IQ in original analyses.

	Original Discriminant Function (Chapter 3)	Discriminant Function Using Only Complete Cases for Variable 3
Study N	430	361
Control N	2,580	2,168
Canonical correlation	.29	.30
Standardized coefficients		
1. Prenatal socioeconomic index	−.44	−.45
2. Male	.39	.38
3. Stanford-Binet IQ	−.35	−.34
4. Parity	.24	.27
5. Apgar score at 5 min.	−.18	−.16
6. Activity level rating	.16	.17
7. Inhalation anesthetics at delivery	.17	.20
8. Maternal heart disease during pregnancy	.16	.20
9. Abnormal speech production (3 yrs.)	.13	.13
10. Edema during pregnancy	.15	.14
11. Number of prenatal visits	−.11	−.07

Table 13
Reliability Coefficients for Seven-Year Achievement and Intelligence Tests

	White		Black	
	Test-Retest	Inter-Observer	Test-Retest	Inter-Observer
WRAT Reading score	.90	.99	.93	.99
Spelling score	.86	.99	.83	.98
Arithmetic score	.77	.99	.79	.99
WISC Full Scale IQ	.85	.99	.80	.99
Verbal IQ	.83	.98	.77	.97
Performance IQ	.72	.99	.66	.99

total number of cases, the minimum complete data count across all discriminators, or a function of the complete data counts (or pair-wise complete counts) for all discriminators, such as some form of average. The total number of cases was used as the sample size because discriminant functions were significant at $p = .0001$ or $p = .00001$ in most cases, and almost always significant at $p = .01$. At these low significance levels, the main purpose of the χ^2 statistic in this study, measuring significance at the .05 level or less, was accomplished equally well by almost any reasonable method of computing sample size.

Reliability of the Criterion Measures. In especially designed "quality control" trials, the reliability of the psychological tests administered at age 7, as well as other examinations in the Collaborative Project, was assessed. Excluding children whose families were identified as uncooperative, a random sample of 400 children was selected for retesting after an interval of approximately 3 months. The sample included 174 white children (83 boys and 91 girls) and 226 black children (111 boys and 115 girls). The retest was conducted by an examiner from a different study center and observed and scored independently by the original examiner. Retests were scheduled throughout each year over a 7-year period.

The most critical measures for this study were the Wide Range Achievement Test scores and the WISC IQ scores. The test–retest and interobserver reliability coefficients are presented in Table 13. Test–retest reliabilities for the Wide Range Achievement Test were highest for the Reading subtest and lowest for the Arithmetic subtest. The WISC reliability coefficients were lower for the Performance Scale IQ than either the Full Scale or Verbal IQ. For the WRAT subtests, the coefficients ranged from .77 to .93. For Full Scale IQ, coefficients were .85 and .80 in the white and black samples, respectively.

3 Risk Factors in Early Development

The independent risk factors for low achievement presented in this chapter were identified in a three-stage analysis conducted in the white and black samples. The significance level adopted at each stage was $p < .05$. Variables assessed from gestation through age 4 were first screened individually. Those that differed between low achievers and controls were categorized as early prenatal demographic, pregnancy and perinatal, infancy, or preschool variables, and discriminant function analyses were performed within each of these four epochs. The results were then entered in a summary analysis across epochs. Certain discriminators not retained in the summary analysis are of considerable interest and are mentioned.

As shown by the size of the standardized coefficients listed in Table 14, the most important early discriminators between low achievers and controls were sex of child in both samples, socioeconomic status and IQ at age 4 among whites and length of labor, maternal parity (number of prior pregnancies), and weight at 1 year among blacks. Considered chronologically, the results of the summary analyses show that in the prenatal period, families of low achievers had a lower socioeconomic index score, reflecting income and occupation and education of head of household, higher maternal parity, and, among blacks, a lower level of maternal education than families of controls. Mothers of low achievers made fewer prenatal clinic visits than mothers of controls. Their pregnancies were more often complicated by heart disease and edema in the white sample and toxemia in the black sample.[1] At delivery, exposure to inhalation anesthetics was more frequent among mothers of low achievers in

[1] Toxemia was defined on the basis of elevated diastolic blood pressure and presence of proteinuria (Friedman & Neff, 1977).

Table 14
Early Discriminators From Gestation to Age Four

Variable	White: Mean or Percent: Low Achievers	White: Mean or Percent: Controls	White: t or χ^2	White: Standardized Coefficient	Black: Mean or Percent: Low Achievers	Black: Mean or Percent: Controls	Black: t or χ^2	Black: Standardized Coefficient
Socioeconomic index	43.4	53.9	10.19*****	−.44	36.1	40.3	5.16*****	−.15
Percent male	69.1%	49.5%	56.04*****	.39	67.2%	45.9%	87.00*****	.64
Stanford-Binet IQ	95.7	101.7	8.48*****	−.35	92.3	95.8	6.20*****	−.21
Parity	2.4	1.9	5.68*****	.24	2.6	2.2	4.79*****	.30
Apgar score (5 min.)	8.7	8.9	2.58**	−.18	9.1	9.1	0.26	—
Inhalation anesthetics at delivery	42.0%	29.4%	26.32*****	.17	42.7%	44.0%	0.29	—
Maternal heart disease during pregnancy	3.1%	1.5%	4.47*	.16	1.4%	1.6%	0.01	—
Activity rating	3.1	3.0	3.18**	.16	3.0	3.0	1.39	—
Edema during pregnancy	48.5%	42.3%	5.42*	.15	23.7%	24.9%	0.29	—
Abnormal speech production (3 yr.)	6.0%	2.5%	7.02**	.13	4.1%	1.6%	7.43**	—
Prenatal visits	8.5	9.8	5.77*****	−.11	7.4	8.2	4.76*****	−.22
Length of 1st stage of labor (hr.)	6.9	7.3	1.51	—	8.2	7.4	2.73**	.32
Weight at 1 yr. (kg)	9.9	9.9	0.20	—	9.5	9.7	3.35***	−.27

(continued)

Table 14 (Continued)

Variable	White				Black			
	Mean or Percent		t or χ^2	Standardized Coefficient	Mean or Percent		t or χ^2	Standardized Coefficient
	Low Achievers	Controls			Low Achievers	Controls		
Abnormal language expression								
(3 yr.)	5.9%	3.6%	<u>2.11</u>	—	6.4%	2.5%	<u>11.38***</u>	.19
Maternal education (yr.)	10.1	10.9	6.81*****	—	10.0	10.5	5.50*****	−.18
Dependency rating	3.3	3.3	0.33	—	3.2	3.1	3.98****	.18
Head circumference in cm								
(4 yr.)	49.9	50.0	0.69	—	49.7	50.0	3.31***	−.16
Toxemia during pregnancy	8.7%	9.8%	<u>0.32</u>	—	11.7%	8.6%	<u>4.83*</u>	.14
Major malformations[a]	3.0%	1.6%	<u>3.26</u>	—	2.1%	1.0%	<u>5.12*</u>	.13
Canonical correlation			.29				.26	
χ^2			266.38*****				281.89*****	
Correct group classification (N)								
Low achievers			(430) 68.4%				(564) 66.7%	
Controls			(2580) 67.1%				(3384) 65.1%	

Note — Chi-square statistic is underlined

[a]Included are malformations of the musculoskeletal, cardiovascular, alimentary and genitourinary systems and of the skin.

*$p < .05$; **$p < .01$; ***$p < .001$; ****$p < .0001$; *****$p < .00001$

the white sample (42 versus 29% of controls). First stage of labor was longer in the black sample even though parity was higher than in controls.

In the newborn period, mean 5-minute Apgar score was slightly lower for white low achievers. Sex of infant was a highly significant discriminator with more than two-thirds of low achievers male as compared with 46 to 50% of controls. Results from pediatric and psychological assessments in the first year of life did not discriminate between groups in the white sample. Black low achievers had a lower mean weight at 1 year of age than controls and a higher frequency of major malformations. At age 3, global ratings of abnormal speech production and abnormal language expression were more frequent among low achievers in the white and black samples, respectively. These problems were detected in approximately 6% of low achievers in each sample.

At 4 years of age, mean IQ scores on the Stanford–Binet were lower for low achievers than controls—96 versus 102 in the white sample and 92 versus 96 in the black sample. The two groups had been matched at age 7 on IQ from the Wechsler Intelligence Scale for Children. Mean scores at that age were 98 in the white sample and 96 in the black sample. On ratings of behavior made by the examining psychologist at age 4, low achievers had slightly higher scores for activity level among whites and for dependency among blacks. Both ratings were close to the average score of three on the five-point scales used. Black low achievers had a slightly smaller head circumference than controls at this age.

All early discriminators had moderate but highly significant correlations of .29 and .26 with the group classification in the white and black samples, respectively. The linear discriminant functions correctly classified approximately two-thirds of low achievers and of controls in both samples. Only three of the variables entered in the summary analyses across epochs were not retained. These were a higher frequency of hospitalization in early pregnancy for mothers of white low achievers ($t = 2.28$, $p < .05$), and lower scores on the 8-month Bayley Motor Scale ($t = 2.01$, $p < .05$) and the 4-year Graham–Ernhart Block Sort Test ($t = 4.84$, $p < .00001$) for black low achievers.

Sex Differences

The underrepresentation of girls among low achievers, as among children classified as learning disabled, dyslexic, or minimally brain damaged, suggests that risk factors for unexpected academic difficulties may differ for boys and girls. The sex differences reported in verbal skills and in aggressive and compliant behaviors (Maccoby & Jacklin, 1974) would predict less successful academic performance for boys than for girls. Low achieving girls, then, may have the more specific and perhaps more severe developmental deficits. In a replication of procedures used for the total group, low achieving boys and girls were compared with same-sex IQ-matched controls on the variables assessed from gestation through age 4. The summary analyses for the white sample are shown in Table 15.

A major discriminator for boys was socioeconomic status of the family, the only variable significant in both sexes. In addition to a lower socioeconomic index score in the prenatal period, mothers of low achieving boys had a higher frequency of edema in pregnancy and smoked more cigarettes daily than mothers of controls. At delivery, they were more frequently exposed to inhalation anesthetics. Other discriminators were from the preschool period and included a higher frequency of abnormal speech production at age 3 and higher failure rates at age 4 on the gross motor task of ball catch and the fine motor task of copying a square. Head circumference at age 4 was slightly smaller for low achieving boys than for controls.

For girls in the white sample, the two most important discriminators were Stanford–Binet IQ at age 4 and socioeconomic status. In the prenatal period, mothers of low achieving girls had a lower socioeconomic index score than mothers of controls, reported retardation among their children more frequently, and were of higher parity and higher prepregnant weight. They had a greater frequency of viral infection in the first trimester of pregnancy and were more often judged to have an inadequate pelvis. The number of prenatal clinic visits made was lower than for mothers of controls. In infancy, low achieving girls had a lower score on the Bayley Mental Scale, and at age 4 their mean IQ was nine points below that of controls.

The canonical correlations and rates of correct classification for the two sexes indicate that early risk factors for low achievement in girls are somewhat better discriminators than those identified for boys. Variables not retained in the summary analyses include some listed in Table 15 because they were significant for the other sex. For boys, differences between the groups in IQ, maternal parity, and number of prenatal visits are in the same direction as for girls. Similarly, for girls, the difference between groups in exposure to inhalation anesthetics parallels that for boys. Other findings from the within-epoch analyses show that low achieving boys were shorter at 1 year of age than controls ($t=2.11$, $p<.05$). Low achieving girls had a higher frequency of maternal anemia during pregnancy than controls ($\chi^2=5.29$, $p<.05$), lower weight at 4 months of age ($t=2.46$, $p<.05$), and a higher frequency of abnormal language reception at age 3 ($\chi^2=4.15$, $p<.05$).

Early discriminators for boys and girls in the black sample are shown in Table 16. Low achievers of both sexes weighed less than controls at 1 year of age and their mothers had made fewer prenatal clinic visits. Discriminators with the largest coefficients were reported retardation in siblings for boys, and for girls, length of labor, language expression at age 3 and attention span at age 4. In the prenatal period mothers of low achieving boys, who reported retarded children in the family more frequently than mothers of controls, also had a lower level of education, higher parity, and a shorter interval since birth of the

Table 15
Sex Differences in Early Discriminators in the White Sample

Variable	Boys				Girls			
	Mean or Percent		t or χ^2	Standardized Coefficient	Mean or Percent		t or χ^2	Standardized Coefficient
	Low Achievers	Controls			Low Achievers	Controls		
Socioeconomic index	44.8	53.9	7.15*****	−.58	40.2	53.9	7.58*****	−.42
Abnormal speech production (3 yr.)	8.2%	3.3%	6.10*	.37	1.3%	1.7%	0.08	—
Failure on ball catch	49.4%	36.5%	12.85***	.34	37.6%	38.1%	0.00	—
Failure to copy square	96.5%	91.0%	6.77*	.26	89.9%	87.9%	0.18	—
Inhalation anesthetics at delivery	41.4%	29.5%	15.30****	.24	43.4%	29.4%	10.16**	—
Edema during pregnancy	50.5%	43.0%	5.01*	.23	44.1%	41.6%	0.21	—
Cigarettes per day in pregnancy	11.1	9.0	2.82**	.22	8.2	9.0	0.82	—
Head circumference in cm (4 yr.)	50.2	50.5	2.33*	−.16	49.2	49.4	1.65	—
Stanford-Binet IQ	96.3	100.3	4.42*****	—	94.2	103.2	7.31*****	−.48
Inadequate pelvis	0.4%	0.5%	0.04	—	3.2%	0.6%	6.70**	.26
Viral infection in 1st trimester	0.7%	1.5%	0.69	—	4.0%	1.2%	4.36*	.26
Prepregnant weight (lb.)	130.6	129.5	0.62	—	134.7	128.1	3.05**	.23
Retardation in older siblings	4.3%	4.6%	0.00	—	9.5%	3.5%	6.90**	.21
Bayley mental score (8 mo.)	79.7	79.6	0.23	—	78.8	80.0	2.31*	−.18

(continued)

Table 15 (Continued)

Variable	Boys				Girls			
	Mean or Percent		t or χ^2	Standardized Coefficient	Mean or Percent		t or χ^2	Standardized Coefficient
	Low Achievers	Controls			Low Achievers	Controls		
Prenatal visits	8.8	9.8	3.71***	—	8.0	9.8	4.73*****	−.16
Parity	2.4	1.8	4.00****	—	2.6	2.0	4.19****	.14
Canonical correlation			.26				.31	
χ^2			109.54*****				141.02*****	
Correct group classification (N)								
Low achievers			(297) 62.0%				(133) 68.4%	
Controls			(1276) 63.2%				(1304) 73.4%	

$*p < .05$; $**p < .01$; $***p < .001$; $****p < .0001$; $*****p < .00001$

Table 16
Sex Differences in Early Discriminators in the Black Sample

Variable	Boys: Mean or Percent: Low Achievers	Boys: Mean or Percent: Controls	Boys: t or χ^2	Boys: Standardized Coefficient	Girls: Mean or Percent: Low Achievers	Girls: Mean or Percent: Controls	Girls: t or χ^2	Girls: Standardized Coefficient
Retardation in older siblings	8.0%	3.2%	9.51**	.34	2.7%	4.1%	0.23	—
Maternal education (yr.)	10.1	10.6	4.84*****	−.28	9.9	10.4	3.30***	—
Weight in kg (1 yr.)	9.6	10.0	4.63*****	−.26	9.1	9.4	3.32***	−.26
Parity	2.7	2.1	4.50*****	.25	2.6	2.2	2.20*	—
Pregnancy-free interval (yr.)	1.6	2.0	2.35*	−.24	1.8	1.9	0.30	—
Head circumference in cm (1 yr.)	45.9	46.3	4.51*****	−.24	45.1	45.3	1.50	—
Stanford-Binet IQ	92.6	95.1	3.50***	−.23	91.7	96.4	4.93*****	—
Toxemia in pregnancy	11.2%	7.7%	4.03*	.22	12.8%	9.3%	1.70	—
Social response to mother rating (8 mo.)	3.3	3.2	2.25*	.22	3.3	3.2	1.33	—
Prenatal visits	7.5	8.2	3.52***	−.20	7.2	8.2	3.41***	−.24
Urinary tract infection during pregnancy	26.4%	20.6%	4.68*	.15	20.4%	24.1%	0.84	—
Head circumference in cm (4 yr.)	49.9	50.3	3.80***	−.10	49.4	49.8	2.53*	—
Length of 1st stage of labor (hr.)	7.8	7.5	0.95	—	8.8	7.3	3.07**	.39
Abnormal language expression (3 yr.)	5.8%	3.2%	2.44	—	7.5%	1.9%	8.98**	.37

(continued)

Table 16 (Continued)

Variable	Boys				Girls			
	Mean or Percent		t or χ^2	Standardized Coefficient	Mean or Percent		t or χ^2	Standardized Coefficient
	Low Achievers	Controls			Low Achievers	Controls		
Attention span rating	2.8	2.8	1.44	—	2.7	2.9	4.20****	−.34
Syphilis during pregnancy	2.5%	3.1%	0.20	—	5.6%	2.6%	4.18*	.30
Verbal communication rating	2.8	2.9	0.55	—	2.7	3.0	3.91****	−.29
Dependency rating	3.1	3.1	1.58	—	3.3	3.1	4.51*****	.26
Socioeconomic index	36.5	40.7	4.11****	—	35.3	39.9	3.37***	−.23
Unfavorable emotional environment (1 yr.)	1.4%	1.9%	0.23	—	5.1%	1.7%	7.35**	.20
Canonical correlation			.24				.25	
χ^2			111.50*****				129.34*****	
Correct group classification (N)								
Low achievers			(379) 55.7%				(185) 50.8%	
Controls			(1554) 65.6%				(1830) 73.9%	

*$p < .05$; **$p < .01$; ***$p < .001$; ****$p < .0001$; *****$p < .00001$

last child. They had made fewer prenatal clinic visits than mothers of control boys and the pregnancy complications of toxemia and urinary tract infection were more frequent. As infants, low achieving boys were rated as more demanding of their mothers during the 8-month psychological examination. Weight at 1 year and head circumference measurements at 1 and 4 years of age were below those for control boys. Mean IQ at age 4 was slightly lower than the control group mean.

Families of low achieving black girls had a lower socioeconomic index score in the prenatal period than families of controls. Pregnancies were more often complicated by syphilis, and fewer prenatal clinic visits were made. First stage of labor was longer than for mothers of controls although parity was significantly higher in the univariate screen. At 1 year of age, low achieving girls weighed less than controls and were more often judged to have an unfavorable emotional environment on the medical summary of the first year of life. At age 3, 7.5% of low achieving girls compared with 2% of controls received abnormal ratings on language expression. On the psychological examination at age 4, they were rated as less attentive, less verbal, and more dependent than control girls.

Canonical correlations between the discriminators and the group classification were highly similar for boys ($R = .24$) and girls ($R = .25$) in the black sample. In both sexes correct classification rates were higher for controls than for low achievers. Three discriminators not retained in the summary analyses appear in Table 16. Group differences in the socioeconomic index score among boys and in maternal education and IQ at age 4 among girls were in the same direction as in the opposite sex sample. Not shown are smaller head circumference measurements for low achieving boys at birth ($t = 3.00$, $p < .01$) and at 4 months of age ($t = 3.86$, $p < .001$), and a lower fetal heart rate in second stage of labor for low achieving girls ($t = 2.27$, $p < .05$).

Summary

Many independent risk factors for low achievement were identified in the period from gestation through age 4. Across ethnic and sex groups the most consistent discriminators were IQ at age 4 and the three maternal characteristics of socioeconomic status, parity, and amount of prenatal care received. In the total white and black samples, sex ratio was a highly significant discriminator. The two ethnic groups differed in the specific complications of pregnancy and delivery related to low achievement. They also differed in that level of maternal education and physical growth measurements were significant for blacks and socioeconomic status as reflected in the socioeconomic index score was relatively more important for whites. Sex differences were identified in both ethnic groups. Among whites, speech and motor skills discriminated for boys, whereas infant and preschool cognitive levels and retardation in siblings were significant for girls. In the black sample, retarded siblings and a smaller head circumference were risk factors for boys. Length of labor, quality of the environment in the first year, and behavior at age 4 discriminated for girls. In the next chapter, characteristics of low achievers at age 7 are presented.

4 Psychological, Physical, and Family Characteristics at School Age

Correlates or markers of low achievement at age 7 were identified in the same sequence of analyses as were the early risk factors. The data base consisted of the psychological and pediatric-neurological examinations administered at this age and a demographic-family history interview conducted with the mother or other caretaker. The medical and social data included events that occurred between ages 1 and 7 years as well as current findings. Test scores, behavior ratings, and examination and interview items were screened individually in the white and black samples. Those that differed between low achievers and controls were entered in the appropriate discriminant function analysis of psychological, pediatric, or demographic and family variables. The significant discriminators were then combined and a summary analysis was run for each ethnic group. The significance level was $p < .05$ throughout. Following an examination of sex differences at age 7, the results of combining risk factors and markers in a single analysis are presented. The effects of study center differences between low achievers and controls were evaluated by repeating this final discriminant analysis with the institutions that passed a univariate screen included.

Table 17 shows the independent discriminators between low achievers and controls in the white and black samples. Variables were retained from each of the three types of data collected at age 7. In addition to sex of child, entered as a control variable, the most important differences between groups were in family size in both samples, score on the Draw-A-Person test and rating of rapport with the examiner among whites, and score on the Bender–Gestalt Test and a global rating of behavior among blacks. Grouping all discriminators by type, those from the psychological examination showed that low achievers were

Table 17
Discriminators at Age Seven

Variable	White				Black			
	Mean or Percent		t or χ^2	Standardized Coefficient	Mean or Percent		t or χ^2	Standardized Coefficient
	Low Achievers	Controls			Low Achievers	Controls		
Percent male	69.1%	49.5%	56.04*****	.36	67.2%	45.9%	87.00*****	.55
Rapport with examiner rating	3.0	2.8	3.68***	.28	2.9	2.9	0.28	—
Draw-A-Person score	90.4	94.6	7.02*****	−.27	93.3	95.2	3.35***	—
Family size	4.5	3.9	5.18*****	.26	4.8	4.1	5.68*****	.30
Socioeconomic index	44.0	53.7	8.51*****	−.23	36.6	41.5	5.43*****	—
Mental illness in study child	1.9%	0.2%	14.56***	.23	0.2%	0.2%	0.24	—
Suspect or abnormal behavior rating	22.6%	10.5%	49.22*****	.21	12.4%	4.9%	47.13*****	.31
Tactile Finger Recognition, left	4.6	4.7	5.29*****	−.20	4.6	4.6	1.66	—
Maternal education (yr.)	10.2	11.1	7.20*****	−.19	10.3	10.7	4.95*****	—
Right-left confusion	30.6%	19.5%	26.44*****	.17	23.7%	20.1%	3.42	—
Self-confidence rating	2.7	2.8	3.63***	−.17	2.8	2.9	2.46*	—
Household moves	3.5	2.6	5.29*****	.16	2.2	1.9	4.63*****	.25
Left dominance	5.1%	2.4%	8.66**	.15	3.9%	2.7%	2.27	—
Goal orientation rating	2.8	2.9	6.16*****	−.15	2.9	3.0	4.08****	−.12

(continued)

Table 17 (Continued)

Variable	White				Black			
	Mean or Percent				Mean or Percent			
	Low Achievers	Controls	t or χ^2	Standardized Coefficient	Low Achievers	Controls	t or χ^2	Standardized Coefficient
Day care	61.4%	53.7%	8.04**	.14	76.4%	77.4%	0.19	—
Younger siblings	0.9	1.0	1.99*	−.13	0.8	0.8	0.68	—
"Hypoxia" without unconsciousness	1.2%	0.3%	4.37*	.11	0.0%	0.1%	0.02	—
Bender-Gestalt error score	7.2	6.2	6.58*****	—	8.4	7.4	7.37*****	.30
Auditory-Vocal Association score (mo.)	80.9	84.2	5.83*****	—	74.0	76.8	6.20*****	−.21
Head circumference in cm	51.3	51.3	0.96	—	51.1	51.3	3.16**	−.21
Father absent	26.5%	17.3%	19.05****	—	49.0%	39.2%	16.93****	.17
Assertiveness rating	3.2	3.2	1.79	—	3.3	3.2	2.39*	.16
Abnormal reflexes	18.5%	13.9%	5.83*	—	14.9%	10.9%	6.95**	.14
Impaired position sense	1.2%	1.2%	0.01	—	1.5%	0.5%	5.93*	.14
Severe burns	0.7%	0.5%	0.02	—	1.8%	0.5%	11.97***	.14
Hemoglobinopathy	0.2%	0.1%	0.01	—	1.3%	0.5%	4.41*	.13
Canonical correlation			.34				.28	
χ^2			371.85*****				327.72*****	
Correct group classification (N)								
Low achievers			(430) 67.0%				(564) 61.9%	
Controls			(2580) 72.1%				(3384) 68.7%	

*$p < .05$; **$p < .01$; ***$p < .001$; ****$p < .0001$; *****$p < .00001$

more often rated as suspect or abnormal in behavior and as less goal oriented than controls. White low achievers had a lower standard score on the Draw-A-Person test, less accurate recognition of tactile stimulation to fingers of the left hand, a greater friendliness toward the examiner, and less self-confidence than controls. Black low achievers had a higher Koppitz error score on the Bender–Gestalt Test, a lower language age on the Auditory–Vocal Association Test, and were less assertive (a higher rating) than controls.

All significant medical findings at age 7 differed by ethnic group. The neurological soft signs of right–left confusion in identifying parts of the body, and left dominance of hand, eye, and foot (not always recognized as a developmental "sign") were more frequent among low achievers in the white sample. Black low achievers had higher frequencies of hypoactive, hyperactive, or asymmetric reflexes and impaired position sense of placement of the great toe or fingers. From interval medical histories, more "hypoxic" episodes were reported for low achievers in the white sample and more burns requiring hospitalization for those in the black sample. Black low achievers had a higher frequency of laboratory-confirmed hemoglobinopathy than controls and a slightly smaller head circumference at age 7.

From the demographic and family history data, a larger number of siblings at age 7 and more frequent household moves since infancy characterized low achievers in both samples. Other discriminators among whites were a lower socioeconomic index score at age 7 for low achievers, less maternal education, more frequent maternal reports of mental illness in the study child, fewer younger siblings, and greater utilization of day care than in controls. More frequent absence of the father at age 7, significant for whites in the univariate screen only, discriminated between low achievers and controls in the black sample.

The canonical correlations of 7-year discriminators with the group classification were .34 and .28 in the white and black samples, respectively, with approximately two-thirds of the low achievers correctly classified. These results are similar to those obtained with early risk factors. Not retained in the summary analysis in the white sample were scores on the Bender–Gestalt and Auditory–Vocal Association Tests, and abnormal reflexes. Group differences on these variables paralleled those in the black sample (Table 17). Eliminated from the summary analysis for blacks were a lower rating on emotional responsiveness for low achievers ($t = 2.57, p < .05$), a higher frequency of head trauma ($\chi^2 = 4.15, p < .05$) and, as shown in Table 17, a lower socioeconomic index score at age 7.

Sex Differences

Discriminators for boys and girls in the white sample are shown in Table 18. Those common to both sexes were performance on the Draw-A-Person and Tactile Finger Recognition tests, a global rating of behavior, right–left confu-

Table 18
Sex Differences in Discriminators at Age Seven in the White Sample

Variable	Boys				Girls			
	Mean or Percent		t or χ^2	Standardized Coefficient	Mean or Percent		t or χ^2	Standardized Coefficient
	Low Achievers	Controls			Low Achievers	Controls		
Self-confidence rating	2.6	2.8	4.05****	−.31	2.8	2.8	0.02	—
Rapport with examiner rating	3.0	2.8	3.56***	.27	2.9	2.8	1.59	—
Maternal education (yr.)	10.3	11.2	5.96*****	−.26	10.0	11.0	4.58*****	—
Family size	4.3	3.9	3.45***	.26	4.7	3.9	4.28****	.26
Day care	64.5%	53.6%	10.45**	.26	54.1%	53.6%	0.00	—
Socioeconomic index	44.8	53.8	6.35*****	−.23	42.1	53.6	5.77*****	−.29
Draw-A-Person score	91.7	95.4	4.88*****	−.22	87.3	93.8	6.26*****	−.36
Household moves	3.5	2.5	4.80*****	.21	3.3	2.6	2.44*	—
Goal orientation rating	2.8	2.9	4.66*****	−.21	2.9	3.0	3.13**	—
Verbal communication rating	2.9	2.8	3.68***	.19	2.8	2.8	0.82	—
Tactile Finger Recognition, left	4.6	4.7	3.12**	−.19	4.5	4.8	3.99****	−.27
Right-left confusion	31.9%	20.8%	15.88****	.19	27.8%	18.2%	6.57*	.16
Head circumference in cm	51.6	51.9	2.91**	−.15	50.5	50.8	2.12*	—
Suspect or abnormal behavior rating	23.6%	13.3%	19.14****	.13	20.3%	7.8%	21.50*****	.28

(continued)

Table 18 (Continued)

Variable	Boys				Girls			
	Mean or Percent		t or χ^2	Standardized Coefficient	Mean or Percent		t or χ^2	Standardized Coefficient
	Low Achievers	Controls			Low Achievers	Controls		
Mental illness in study child	1.4%	0.3%	2.20	—	3.2%	0.1%	14.88***	.36
Salicylate intoxication	0.3%	0.6%	0.00	—	2.3%	0.1%	9.86**	.27
Bender-Gestalt error score	7.0	6.2	4.29****	—	7.6	6.1	5.35*****	.19
Retardation in siblings	12.1%	7.7%	5.05*	—	18.7%	8.2%	13.46***	.17
Canonical correlation			.33				.32	
χ^2			180.23*****				158.99*****	
Correct group classification (N)								
Low achievers			(297) 64.0%				(133) 61.7%	
Controls			(1276) 68.0%				(1304) 78.7%	

$^{*}p < .05$; $^{**}p < .01$; $^{***}p < .001$; $^{****}p < .0001$; $^{*****}p < .00001$

sion, family size, and socioeconomic status. The three psychological variables were more important for girls than boys as indicated by their standardized coefficients. Discriminators unique to boys were four individual behavior ratings (self-confidence, rapport with the examiner, goal orientation, and verbal communication), head circumference at age 7, maternal education, day care, and number of household moves. Head circumference was significant for girls in an intermediate discriminant function analysis, and goal orientation, maternal education, and household moves were significant for girls in the initial univariate screen. Mental illness as reported by the caretaker and a history of salicylate intoxication were relatively important, unique discriminators for girls. A higher error score on the Bender–Gestalt Test and retarded younger siblings, reported more than twice as frequently for low achieving girls than controls, were significant for boys in the univariate screen only.

Canonical correlations and rates of correct classification were similar for the two sexes. The most accurately classified subgroup was the control girls. Characteristics of low achievers not retained in the summary analyses were a lower score on the Auditory–Vocal Association Test for both boys ($t=4.18$, $p<.0001$) and girls ($t=4.62$, $p<.00001$), and, for girls, a shorter attention span ($t=3.14$, $p<.01$), smaller head circumference (Table 18), and higher frequency of younger half-siblings in the family ($t=3.11$, $p<.01$).

In the black sample, low achievers of both sexes were rated as suspect or abnormal in behavior more frequently than controls (Table 19). They had poorer scores on the Bender–Gestalt and Auditory–Vocal Association Tests, a higher frequency of severe burns, and had experienced more household moves. The latter variable was relatively more important for boys and the psychological measures, particularly performance on the Bender, were more important for girls. Other discriminators differed in the two groups. Low achieving boys had a shorter attention span, smaller head circumference, higher frequencies of head trauma and of maternal mental illness (as reported by the mother), and *less* poor coordination than controls. The larger family size of low achieving boys, an important discriminator, and a lower level of maternal education were significant for girls in the univariate screen only. Unique to low achieving girls were a lower Draw-A-Person score (significant for boys in the univariate screen), less emotional responsiveness, higher frequencies of abnormal reflexes and of infectious and noninfectious skin conditions, and a higher paternal age than controls.

Canonical correlations between 7-year discriminators and the group classification were .29 for boys and .24 for girls. In both groups, approximately 55% of low achievers and 70% of controls were correctly classified. Not retained in the summary analyses were a more frequent absence of the father among low achieving black boys ($\chi^2=8.80$, $p<.01$), and, among girls, a higher frequency of right–left confusion ($\chi^2=5.03$, $p<.05$) and a lower socioeconomic index score ($t=3.52$, $p<.001$).

Table 19
Sex Differences in Discriminators at Age Seven in the Black Sample

Variable	Boys				Girls			
	Mean or Percent		t or χ^2	Standardized Coefficient	Mean or Percent		t or χ^2	Standardized Coefficient
	Low Achievers	Controls			Low Achievers	Controls		
Head circumference in cm	51.1	51.6	5.78*****	−.44	51.0	51.1	0.22	—
Family size	4.8	4.1	5.48*****	.36	4.6	4.2	2.33*	—
Household moves	2.3	1.8	4.31****	.36	2.2	1.9	2.03*	.25
Suspect or abnormal behavior rating	12.7%	5.8%	20.69*****	.28	11.9%	4.1%	20.11*****	.33
Bender-Gestalt error score	8.1	7.1	5.50*****	.22	9.1	7.6	6.20*****	.41
Attention span rating	2.9	3.0	3.69***	−.22	2.9	3.0	1.26	—
Auditory-Vocal Association score	74.2	76.8	4.34****	−.20	73.4	76.9	4.44*****	−.31
Poor coordination	3.8%	6.7%	3.86*	−.19	3.4%	3.1%	0.00	—
Maternal education (yr.)	10.3	10.8	4.50*****	−.18	10.2	10.7	2.75**	—
Head trauma	1.7%	0.4%	5.54*	.16	0.0%	0.3%	0.00	—
Maternal mental illness	6.6%	3.6%	4.75*	.16	5.4%	4.4%	0.13	—
Severe burns	1.9%	0.6%	3.92*	.14	1.7%	0.3%	4.89*	.17

(continued)

Table 19 (Continued)

Variable	Boys				Girls			
	Mean or Percent		t or χ^2	Standardized Coefficient	Mean or Percent		t or χ^2	Standardized Coefficient
	Low Achievers	Controls			Low Achievers	Controls		
Paternal age (yr.)	35.9	35.5	0.70	—	37.5	35.6	2.03*	.32
Skin infections	3.4%	3.5%	0.01	—	6.9%	2.5%	9.21**	.27
Skin conditions	10.1%	12.4%	1.25	—	18.0%	10.6%	8.03**	.24
Draw-A-Person score	94.8	96.7	2.56*	—	90.2	94.0	4.37****	−.22
Emotionality rating	2.8	2.9	1.49	—	2.8	2.9	2.02*	−.21
Abnormal reflexes	13.6%	11.4%	1.15	—	17.4%	10.4%	7.42**	.21
Canonical correlation			.29				.24	
χ^2			173.05*****				118.61*****	
Correct group classification (N)								
Low achievers			(379) 55.7%				(185) 54.6%	
Controls			(1554) 68.9%				(1830) 72.4%	

*$p < .05$; **$p < .01$; ***$p < .001$; ****$p < .0001$; *****$p < .00001$

All Discriminators

Early risk factors and the later markers of low achievement were analyzed together to evaluate their combined and individual effectiveness as discriminators between groups over the total developmental span from gestation to age 7. Standardized coefficients (negative when the value for low achievers is lower than controls) and summary statistics for the combined analysis in each sample are shown in Table 20. Approximately 75% of the risk factors and 67 to 85% of the markers (the higher figure among blacks) were retained as independent discriminators. The canonical correlations were only slightly higher than those obtained in the analyses of risk factors or markers alone ($R = .36$ versus .29 and .34 in the white sample; $R = .31$ versus .26 and .28 in the black sample). Rates of correct classification of low achievers and controls remained essentially the same across the three analyses.

Differences in the antecedents and correlates of low achievement in the two ethnic groups are immediately apparent from inspection of the results presented in Table 20. Number of prenatal visits, sex ratio, and a global rating of behavior at age 7 were the only common discriminators. Maternal education was retained in both samples but as a 7-year marker for whites and a prenatal risk factor for blacks. Risk factors no longer significant in the white sample were edema in pregnancy, speech production at age 3, and activity level at age 4. Four demographic markers (family size, socioeconomic status at age 7, household moves, and number of younger siblings) and a history of hypoxia were also eliminated. Not retained for blacks were the risk factors of parity, socioeconomic status in the prenatal period, and IQ score at age 4. Marker variables eliminated were goal orientation and head circumference at age 7. The top-ranking discriminators in both samples were sex of child, psychological markers including ratings of behavior and scores on the Draw-A-Person and Bender–Gestalt tests, prenatal socioeconomic status (whites), and family size (blacks).

These analyses were repeated with study centers that contributed different proportions of low achievers and controls included. Residual variation in study populations or differences in procedures among these unequally represented centers could account for some of the findings. Those that were overrepresented among low achievers compared with controls were Providence, Johns Hopkins, and, in the white sample, Oregon (Table 1, Appendix 4). Underrepresented centers were Boston in both samples, Buffalo and Minnesota in the white sample, and Virginia in the black sample. Entry of these variables in the final discriminant analyses produced only minimal changes, the largest being the elimination of maternal education as a 7-year marker in the white sample (Table 2, Appendix 4). The three overrepresented institutions were retained as independent discriminators for whites and an underrepresented one for blacks. The canonical correlations were virtually unchanged from the original analyses indicating no increase in explanatory power as a result of adding the study centers.

Table 20
All Discriminators Between Low Achievers and Controls

	Standardized Coefficient	
	White	Black
Percent male	.31	.54
Rapport with examiner rating (7 yr.)	.28	—
Socioeconomic index (prenatal)	−.26	—
Draw-A-Person score	−.23	—
Mental illness in study child	.22	—
Suspect or abnormal behavior rating (7 yr.)	.21	.26
Parity	.19	—
Stanford-Binet IQ	−.19	—
Tactile Finger Recognition, left	−.19	—
Right-left confusion	.16	—
Inhalation anesthetics at delivery	.15	—
Self-confidence rating (7 yr.)	−.15	—
Goal orientation rating (7 yr.)	−.14	—
Apgar score (5 min.)	−.14	—
Day care	.14	—
Left dominance	.13	—
Maternal heart disease during pregnancy	.11	—
Maternal education	−.11[a]	−.14[b]
Prenatal visits	−.09	−.14
Bender-Gestalt error score	—	.26
Family size	—	.24
Length of 1st stage of labor	—	.22
Weight at one year	—	−.20
Household moves	—	.18
Abnormal language expression (3 yr.)	—	.16
Assertiveness rating (7 yr.)	—	.15
Toxemia during pregnancy	—	.14
Dependency rating (4 yr.)	—	.14
Auditory-Vocal Association score	—	−.14
Severe burns	—	.14
Father absent (7 yr.)	—	.13
Head circumference (4 yr.)	—	−.12
Impaired position sense	—	.12
Hemoglobinopathy	—	.12
Abnormal reflexes	—	.12
Major malformations	—	.10

(continued)

Table 20 (Continued)

	Standardized Coefficient	
	White	Black
Canonical correlation	.36	.31
χ^2	417.44*	404.09*
Correct group classification (N)		
Low achievers	(430) 67.9%	(564) 63.8%
Controls	(2580) 72.7%	(3384) 70.6%

[a] At seven-year interview
[b] At prenatal interview
$*p < .00001$

The combined analyses for boys and girls in each sample are shown in Tables 21 and 22. The retention of risk factors and markers differed by sex with more of the early discriminators retained for girls in the white and black samples (100 and 90% versus 63 and 42% for boys) and more marker variables retained for boys (79 and 83% versus 50 and 73% for girls). Canonical correlations were slightly higher than those for risk factors or markers in all groups. Among boys, a slight linear increase was noted across the early, late, and total periods (e.g., $R = .26$, .33, and .36 in the white sample) but not among girls (e.g., $R = .25$, .24, and .31 in the black sample). As in the two earlier analyses, the most accurately classified subgroups were the control girls.

In the white sample, low achievers of both sexes shared the prenatal risk factor of lower socioeconomic status and the 7-year markers of lower scores on the Draw-A-Person and Tactile Finger Recognition tests and higher frequencies of suspect or abnormal behavior. Risk factors omitted for boys were maternal smoking in pregnancy and, at age 4, copying a square and head circumference. Seven-year variables omitted were socioeconomic status, maternal education, and household moves for boys, and the Bender score, right–left confusion, family size, and retarded siblings for girls. The most important discriminators were prenatal socioeconomic status in both sexes, early speech production and later behavior ratings and day care for boys, and IQ at age 4, reported mental illness, and score on the Draw-A-Person test for girls.

Study center differences between low achieving boys and girls in the white sample and their respective controls resembled those in the total sample except that differences between groups in the underrepresented centers of Minnesota for boys and Buffalo for girls were insignificant. The effect of entering five centers in the final discriminant analysis for boys was the removal of edema in pregnancy as a risk factor (Table 3, Appendix 4). One of three overrepresented centers was retained as an independent discriminator. Effects were larger for girls with three of five study centers retained and the risk factors of prenatal socioeconomic status and the Bayley mental score dropped from the analysis. A comparison of the canonical correlation with those in the original analyses showed little or no change.

In the black sample, boys and girls had a common risk factor of less prenatal care and common markers of lower scores on the Bender and Auditory–Vocal Association tests and a higher frequency of suspect or abnormal behavior.

Table 21
Sex Differences in All Discriminators in the White Sample

	Standardized Coefficient	
	Boys	Girls
Socioeconomic index (prenatal)	−.36	−.28
Self-confidence rating (7 yr.)	−.29	—
Rapport with examiner rating (7 yr.)	.26	—
Abnormal speech production (3 yr.)	.24	—
Day care	.24	—
Goal orientation rating (7 yr.)	−.21	—
Family size	.21	—
Failure on ball catch	.21	—
Inhalation anesthetics at delivery	.21	—
Right-left confusion	.19	—
Draw-A-Person score	−.18	−.29
Verbal communication rating (7 yr.)	.18	—
Head circumference (7 yr.)	−.17	—
Suspect or abnormal behavior rating (7 yr.)	.14	.25
Edema during pregnancy	.13	—
Tactile Finger Recognition, left	−.13	−.23
Stanford-Binet IQ	—	−.29
Mental illness in study child	—	.29
Inadequate pelvis	—	.25
Salicylate intoxication	—	.24
Viral infection in 1st trimester	—	.21
Pre-pregnant weight	—	.18
Retardation in older siblings	—	.17
Prenatal visits	—	−.15
Parity	—	.14
Bayley mental score (8 mo.)	—	−.09
Canonical correlation	.36	.38
χ^2	211.11*	224.49*
Correct group classification (N)		
Low achievers	(297) 66.0%	(133) 61.7%
Controls	(1276) 68.4%	(1304) 80.6%

*$p < .00001$

Table 22
Sex Differences in All Discriminators in the Black Sample

	Standardized Coefficient	
	Boys	Girls
Head circumference (7 yr.)	−.41	—
Household moves	.33	—
Family size	.31	—
Suspect or abnormal behavior rating (7 yr.)	.25	.21
Retardation in older siblings	.22	—
Bender-Gestalt error score	.22	.30
Auditory-Vocal Association score	−.22	−.14
Attention span rating (7 yr.)	−.21	—
Social response to mother rating (8 mo.)	.20	—
Poor coordination	−.20	—
Head trauma	.17	—
Pregnancy-free interval	−.14	—
Urinary tract infection during pregnancy	.14	—
Maternal mental illness	.12	—
Prenatal visits	−.10	−.22
Length of 1st stage of labor	—	.32
Abnormal language expression (3 yr.)	—	.28
Skin infections	—	.24
Paternal age	—	.23
Attention span rating (4 yr.)	—	−.23
Weight at one year	—	−.22
Verbal communication rating (4 yr.)	—	−.20
Dependency rating (4 yr.)	—	.18
Syphilis during pregnancy	—	.18
Skin conditions	—	.17
Unfavorable emotional environment (1 yr.)	—	.16
Severe burns	—	.15
Abnormal reflexes	—	.14
Canonical correlation	.31	.31
χ^2	189.28*	198.44*
Correct group classification (N)		
Low achievers	(379) 60.7%	(185) 57.8%
Controls	(1554) 69.4%	(1830) 76.8%

*$p < .00001$

Several risk factors were eliminated for boys including maternal education, parity, toxemia, head circumference measurements at 1 and 4 years (supplanted by the one at age 7), weight at 1 year, and IQ at age 4. Prenatal socioeconomic status was not retained for girls. Seven-year markers no longer significant were maternal education and severe burns for boys, and Draw-A-Person score, emotionality rating, and household moves for girls. The most important discriminators for boys were head circumference, household moves, and family size, all at age 7. For girls, they were the risk factors of length of labor and early language expression and the 7-year Bender score. Study center differences had little or no effect on these results. One of three centers was retained for boys producing only minimal changes in some coefficients and no change in the canonical correlation (Table 4, Appendix 4). The two centers entered for girls were not retained in the analysis.

Summary

Independent correlates of low achievement were identified from the psychological, medical, and demographic–family history data collected at age 7. They included perceptual motor and behavioral deficits, minor neurological signs, and larger and less stable families. Both ethnic group and sex differences were found in specific markers of low achievement. All discriminators combined from gestation through age 7 had only a slightly higher canonical correlation with the group classification than risk factors or markers alone. In each sample, early risk factors were better discriminators for girls than boys. Study center differences between low achievers and controls were found to have little effect on the results of the combined discriminant analyses.

5 The Lower Achieving Subgroup

Among several subgroups of low achievers selected for study, the first was children with deficits in both reading and spelling. Their grade ratings in both areas on the Wide Range Achievement Test were more than 1 year below grade placement, or for repeaters, no higher than grade placement. Greater homogeneity was predicted in this more academically impaired subgroup than in the larger group where a deficit in only one area was required. The proportion of low achievers meeting the subgroup criteria was 36% in the white sample (156/430) and 30% in the black sample (172/564). They were compared with IQ-matched controls of the same ethnic group who were at least at grade level in reading, spelling, and arithmetic. Analyses were performed in the same sequence as described earlier beginning with a univariate screen. The summary discriminant function analyses of risk factors, markers, and all discriminators are presented for each subgroup and for boys and girls.

Early Risk Factors

Discriminators from the period of gestation through age 4 are shown in Table 23. In the white subgroup, a higher frequency of major malformations in infancy was the only unique risk factor. These included musculoskeletal and genitourinary abnormalities, cleft lip, and cavernous hemanigioma. Other characteristics from the prenatal, perinatal, and preschool periods were shared with the larger group of low achievers in the white sample. The most important discriminators were sex of child, prenatal socioeconomic status, maternal heart disease in pregnancy, and IQ at age 4. Unique to the black subgroup were absence of the father in the prenatal period, maternal smoking in pregnancy,

Table 23
Early Discriminators from Gestation to Age Four in the Lower Achieving Subgroup

Variable	White				Black			
	Mean or Percent				Mean or Percent			
	LA Subgroup	Controls	t or χ^2	Standardized Coefficient	LA Subgroup	Controls	t or χ^2	Standardized Coefficient
Percent male	71.2%	49.6%	26.79*****	.42	72.7%	46.8%	42.71*****	.57
Socioeconomic index	43.7	54.2	6.38*****	−.38	34.8	39.8	3.66***	—
Maternal heart disease during pregnancy	4.6%	1.4%	8.14**	.31	1.2%	1.6%	0.02	—
Stanford-Binet IQ	95.7	101.9	5.28*****	−.30	90.9	95.5	4.91*****	−.31
Inhalation anesthetics at delivery	45.5%	29.2%	17.70****	.24	42.9%	43.8%	0.02	—
Prenatal visits	8.0	9.8	5.02*****	−.22	7.2	8.2	3.45***	−.11
Major malformations	4.5%	1.8%	4.38*	.22	2.3%	1.2%	0.99	—
Parity	2.5	1.9	3.74***	.20	2.9	2.2	3.91****	.35
Abnormal language expression (3 yr.)	8.7%	3.7%	3.15	—	8.3%	2.3%	10.78**	.32
Head circumference in cm (4 yr.)	49.9	50.0	0.26	—	49.6	50.0	2.92**	−.30
Father absent	18.4%	13.1%	3.05	—	46.1%	34.6%	8.71**	.25

(continued)

Table 23 (Continued)

Variable	White				Black			
	Mean or Percent		t or χ^2	Standardized Coefficient	Mean or Percent		t or χ^2	Standardized Coefficient
	LA Subgroup	Controls			LA Subgroup	Controls		
Cigarettes per day in pregnancy	10.2	9.0	2.02*	—	5.2	3.5	3.13**	.24
Prior fetal death	8.6%	14.2%	2.69	—	7.4%	15.2%	5.05*	−.20
Social response to mother rating (8 mo.)	3.3	3.2	0.77	—	3.4	3.3	2.31*	.19
Canonical correlation			.19				.21	
χ^2			117.71*****				144.66*****	
Correct group classification (N)								
LA subgroup			(156) 69.9%				(172) 68.0%	
Controls			(2964) 68.7%				(3096) 70.1%	

$^{*}p < .05$; $^{**}p < .01$; $^{***}p < .001$; $^{****}p < .0001$; $^{*****}p < .00001$

fewer maternal reports of prior fetal death, and a higher rating for interaction with the mother at age 8 months. Discriminators with the largest coefficients were sex of child, parity, and IQ at age 4, all significant in the white subgroup, and language expression at age 3 and head circumference at age 4. An additional common discriminator was number of prenatal visits.

Canonical correlations of .19 and .21 indicate only modest relationships between the early discriminators and the subgroup classification. Risk factors identified earlier but not retained in the summary analysis for whites were a higher frequency of maternal hypotension in pregnancy ($\chi^2=4.89$, $p<.05$) and a higher activity level rating at age 4 ($t=2.25$, $p<.05$). Not retained in the black subgroup were a lower level of maternal education in the prenatal period ($t=3.75$, $p<.001$) and a lower rating on verbal communication at age 4 ($t=3.07$, $p<.01$).

Boys and girls in each subgroup were compared with same-sex controls. Risk factors for the two sexes in the white subgroup are shown in Table 24. The only common discriminator was number of prenatal visits. With the exception of inhalation anesthetics at delivery, all discriminators for boys in the subgroup differed from those for boys in the larger group. Maternal educational level and mean score on a nonverbal intelligence test (SRA) were lower than in controls. Hypotension in pregnancy was more frequent and fewer prenatal visits were made. During labor and delivery, exposure to inhalation anesthetics was greater, and one of four fetal heart rate measures was higher than in controls. Postnatal discriminators were a smaller head circumference at age 1, and ratings of a shorter attention span and more verbal communication during the psychological examination at age 4.

Subgroup girls shared several discriminators with the total group of girls: lower socioeconomic status in the prenatal period and more frequent reports of retarded older siblings; inadequate pelvis, higher prepregnant weight and fewer prenatal visits; and lower IQ at age 4. Unique discriminators were a higher frequency of maternal retardation (as reported by the mother), third trimester bacterial infection and greater weight gain in pregnancy, a positive Coombs test indicating Rh sensitization in the neonate, major malformations in infancy, and poorer performance on a fine and a gross motor task at age 4.

Risk factors were better discriminators for girls than boys in the white subgroup. Canonical correlations were .29 and .22, respectively, with 67% of subgroup girls and 86% of their controls correctly classified compared with rates of 60 and 71% for boys.

In the black subgroup, the common risk factor for boys and girls was lower IQ at age 4 (Table 25). Among boys, three of nine early discriminators were unique to the subgroup: absence of the father in the prenatal period, slightly taller mothers, and a higher rating for cooperative behavior at age 4. Other discriminators including the relatively important ones of higher parity and retarded older siblings were significant in the larger group of low achieving

Table 24
Sex Differences in Early Discriminators in the White Lower Achieving Subgroup

Variable	Boys				Girls			
	Mean or Percent		t or χ^2	Standardized Coefficient	Mean or Percent		t or χ^2	Standardized Coefficient
	LA Subgroup	Controls			LA Subgroup	Controls		
Maternal education (yr.)	9.9	11.0	4.83*****	−.36	10.0	10.9	2.50*	—
Inhalation anesthetics at delivery	49.6%	29.6%	18.22****	.36	34.9%	28.7%	0.50	—
Attention span rating	2.6	2.8	3.07**	−.34	2.9	2.9	0.42	—
Verbal communication rating	3.1	2.9	2.27*	.29	2.8	2.9	0.62	—
Hypotension during pregnancy	5.5%	1.8%	4.20*	.29	5.3%	2.4%	0.37	—
Maternal SRA score	38.0	41.3	3.33***	−.27	39.8	40.9	0.80	—
Head circumference in cm (1 yr.)	45.9	46.3	2.65**	−.27	44.8	45.1	1.42	—
Lowest FHR in 1st stage of labor	127.7	124.3	2.13*	.19	125.8	126.8	0.40	—
Prenatal visits	8.2	9.7	3.59***	−.17	7.5	9.8	3.58***	−.21
Inadequate pelvis	0.9%	1.1%	0.14	—	7.1%	0.9%	10.21**	.38
Bacterial infection in 3rd trimester	3.8%	3.1%	0.02	—	11.9%	3.0%	7.81**	.34
Stanford-Binet IQ	96.4	99.9	2.51*	—	93.9	103.8	4.72*****	−.33
Retardation in older siblings	1.3%	4.6%	1.26	—	10.8%	2.9%	4.68*	.24

(continued)

Table 24 (Continued)

Variable	Boys				Girls			
	Mean or Percent		t or χ^2	Standardized Coefficient	Mean or Percent		t or χ^2	Standardized Coefficient
	LA Subgroup	Controls			LA Subgroup	Controls		
Retardation in mother	0.9%	0.8%	0.19	—	4.7%	0.6%	4.64*	.24
Positive Coombs, newborn	0.9%	2.9%	0.82	—	10.3%	3.1%	4.13*	.24
Weight gain during pregnancy (lb.)	23.3	23.4	0.12	—	27.2	23.7	2.43*	.24
Prepregnant weight (lb.)	130.8	128.8	0.78	—	137.2	128.2	2.55*	.23
Failure to hop, right	25.4%	36.6%	3.20	—	38.5%	17.5%	6.21*	.23
Failure on pegboard, left	0.0%	3.7%	2.18	—	9.1%	2.1%	4.37*	.23
Major malformations	2.7%	1.2%	0.83	—	8.9%	2.4%	4.91*	.20
Socioeconomic index	45.2	54.0	4.50*****	—	40.2	54.4	4.69*****	−.16
Canonical correlation			.22				.29	
χ^2			77.27*****				132.63*****	
Correct group classification (N)								
LA subgroup			(111) 60.4%				(45) 66.7%	
Controls			(1469) 70.8%				(1495) 85.9%	

$^*p < .05$; $^{**}p < .01$; $^{***}p < .001$; $^{****}p < .0001$; $^{*****}p < .00001$

Table 25
Sex Differences in Early Discriminators in the Black Lower Achieving Subgroup

Variable	Boys				Girls			
	Mean or Percent		t or χ^2	Standardized Coefficient	Mean or Percent		t or χ^2	Standardized Coefficient
	LA Subgroup	Controls			LA Subgroup	Controls		
Parity	2.9	2.1	3.65***	.39	2.8	2.2	1.84	—
Retardation in older siblings	11.0%	3.5%	7.72**	.39	3.6%	3.9%	0.16	—
Cooperation rating	3.1	3.0	2.33*	.38	2.9	3.0	1.92	—
Stanford-Binet IQ	91.7	94.8	2.75**	−.32	88.7	96.1	4.20****	−.15
Head circumference in cm (4 yr.)	49.8	50.3	2.90**	−.30	49.1	49.8	2.56*	—
Father absent	46.3%	34.0%	6.92**	.29	45.7%	35.2%	1.72	—
Social response to mother rating (8 mo.)	3.4	3.2	2.21*	.27	3.4	3.3	1.19	—
Maternal height (in.)	64.0	63.4	2.40*	.26	63.2	63.6	0.82	—
Prenatal visits	7.1	8.2	3.17**	−.21	7.3	8.1	1.52	—
Abnormal language expression (3 yr.)	7.2%	3.2%	2.00	—	10.7%	1.5%	8.79**	.46
Lowest FHR in 2nd stage of labor	134.7	131.0	1.57	—	123.2	133.1	3.00**	−.43
Maternal seizures in pregnancy	0.0%	0.4%	0.03	—	5.0%	0.5%	7.45**	.37

(continued)

Table 25 (Continued)

Variable	Boys				Girls			
	Mean or Percent				Mean or Percent			
	LA Subgroup	Controls	t or χ^2	Standardized Coefficient	LA Subgroup	Controls	t or χ^2	Standardized Coefficient
Maternal education (yr.)	10.2	10.6	2.34*	—	9.4	10.4	3.79***	−.26
Delayed motor development (1 yr.)	0.8%	0.6%	0.07	—	4.4%	0.4%	6.64**	.25
Cigarettes per day in pregnancy	4.7	3.5	1.90	—	6.5	3.6	2.98**	.21
Failure to copy circle	7.2%	6.5%	0.01	—	12.8%	4.0%	5.32*	.21
Age at menarche (yr.)	12.7	12.6	0.97	—	11.9	12.7	3.40***	−.20
Gestation at registration (wk.)	23.9	22.7	1.75	—	25.5	22.4	2.73**	.19
Major malformations	0.8%	1.4%	0.02	—	6.4%	1.0%	7.66**	.19
Highest FHR in 1st stage of labor	150.3	150.0	0.26	—	146.9	150.7	2.15*	−.08
Canonical correlation		.21				.30		
χ^2		70.02*****				163.71*****		
Correct group classification (N)								
LA subgroup		(125) 56.0%				(47) 46.8%		
Controls		(1450) 72.3%				(1646) 90.2%		

*$p < .05$; **$p < .01$; ***$p < .001$; ****$p < .0001$; *****$p < .00001$

boys. Subgroup girls shared only a higher frequency of abnormal language expression at age 3 with the total group of girls. Discriminating maternal characteristics ascertained in the prenatal period were a lower age at menarche, less education, seizures in pregnancy and heavier smoking, and later registration for prenatal care. During labor, two of four fetal heart rate measures were lower than in controls. Postnatal discriminators in addition to preschool language expression and IQ score were a higher frequency of major malformations, delayed motor development at one year, and failure on a simple copying task at age 4.

Similar to the white subgroup, the canonical correlation between early discriminators and the subgroup classification was higher for girls (.30) than boys (.21). About 90% of control girls but less than 50% of subgroup girls were correctly classified. Corresponding rates for boys were 72 and 56%.

Markers at Age 7

Characteristics of the lower achieving subgroups at school age are shown in Table 26. Variables entered in the summary discriminant function analyses were those that were retained in the three intermediate discriminant analyses of psychological, physical, and demographic-family history data collected at age 7. Among whites, rating of less fearfulness and a higher activity level, reported retardation among siblings, and higher housing density were markers unique to the subgroup. A less frequent occurrence of German measles was also a subgroup characteristic. The most important discriminators were maternal report of mental illness in the child, a global rating of behavior at age 7, and sex ratio. The latter two variables discriminated in the black subgroup also. Other common markers were the self-confidence rating and maternal education.

Markers unique to the black subgroup were lower ratings for attention span, emotionality, and self-confidence, bilateral hearing loss greater than 30 decibels, febrile seizures, and the family characteristics of less maternal education and higher frequencies of both paternal employment and public assistance. Discriminators with the largest coefficients were bilateral hearing impairment and sex ratio.

Summary statistics were similar in the two subgroups. The canonical correlations of .25 were slightly higher than those obtained for early risk factors. Discriminators not retained in the white subgroup included a lower Auditory–Vocal Association score ($t=3.22$, $p<.01$) and a lower Tactile Finger Recognition score on the right hand ($t=3.04$, $p<.01$), abnormal reflexes ($\chi^2=6.18$, $p<.05$), and more frequent household moves ($t=2.67$, $p<.01$). A higher frequency of skin infections in the black subgroup was not retained in the summary analysis ($\chi^2=5.17$, $p<.05$).

Boys and girls in the white subgroup shared the markers of a lower Draw-A-Person score and suspect or abnormal behavior at age 7, and lower so-

Table 26
Discriminators at Age Seven in the Lower Achieving Subgroup

Variable	White				Black			
	Mean or Percent		t or χ^2	Standardized Coefficient	Mean or Percent		t or χ^2	Standardized Coefficient
	LA Subgroup	Controls			LA Subgroup	Controls		
Suspect or abnormal behavior rating	26.3%	10.5%	35.08*****	.34	14.0%	5.1%	22.61*****	.23
Mental illness in study child	4.7%	0.5%	19.29****	.34	0.0%	0.1%	0.96	—
Percent male	71.2%	49.6%	26.79*****	.32	72.7%	46.8%	42.71*****	.43
Fearfulness rating	2.9	3.0	2.49*	−.29	3.0	3.0	1.22	—
Draw-A-Person score	89.7	94.4	5.08*****	−.28	93.8	94.8	1.04	—
Maternal education (yr.)	10.1	11.1	5.07*****	−.28	10.1	10.7	4.00****	−.16
Housing density	1.3	1.2	4.61*****	.27	1.4	1.4	1.04	—
Self-confidence rating	2.6	2.8	2.46*	−.21	2.8	2.9	3.60***	−.17
Retardation in siblings	16.1%	8.1%	10.22**	.17	11.2%	7.4%	2.42	—
Tactile Finger Recognition, left	4.5	4.7	3.21**	−.17	4.6	4.6	0.33	—
Activity rating	3.2	2.9	4.70*****	.17	3.0	3.0	0.14	—
Right-left confusion	31.6%	20.6%	10.12**	.16	24.0%	20.6%	0.89	—
German measles	3.9%	9.0%	4.28*	−.15	4.2%	3.9%	0.00	—
Bilateral hearing impairment	0.0%	0.1%	1.69	—	1.2%	0.0%	12.05***	.36

(continued)

Table 26 (Continued)

Variable	White				Black			
	Mean or Percent		t or χ^2	Standardized Coefficient	Mean or Percent		t or χ^2	Standardized Coefficient
	LA Subgroup	Controls			LA Subgroup	Controls		
Father employed	87.9%	91.2%	0.99	—	98.7%	90.7%	4.68*	.28
Family size	4.5	3.9	3.38***	—	5.1	4.2	4.77*****	.26
Abnormal reflexes	21.3%	13.8%	6.18*	—	21.6%	12.1%	12.05***	.24
Public assistance	29.2%	17.8%	11.14***	—	44.7%	30.0%	14.00***	.23
Household moves	3.2	2.6	2.69**	—	2.4	1.9	4.03****	.22
Attention span rating	2.8	2.9	3.86***	—	2.9	3.0	3.69***	−.22
Emotionality rating	3.0	2.9	2.33*	—	2.8	2.9	3.03**	−.19
Febrile seizures	1.9%	2.2%	0.00	—	5.8%	2.4%	6.32*	.15
Bender-Gestalt error score	7.2	6.2	4.09****	—	8.3	7.5	3.26**	.14
Canonical correlation			.25				.25	
χ^2			192.72*****				207.23*****	
Correct group classification (N)								
LA subgroup			(156) 63.5%				(172) 60.5%	
Controls			(2964) 76.5%				(3096) 75.4%	

$*p < .05$; $**p < .01$; $***p < .001$; $****p < .0001$; $*****p < .00001$

cioeconomic status (Table 27). Characteristics of subgroup boys not identified in the larger group of low achieving boys were less fearfulness and a higher activity level, higher housing density, and reported mental illness of the mother. Discriminators with the largest coefficients were housing density, the fearfulness rating, and a lower rating for self-confidence. For subgroup girls, new markers were a lower Tactile Finger Recognition score on the right hand, a lower Auditory–Vocal Association score, and abnormal reflexes. A global rating of suspect or abnormal behavior was the most important discriminator. As indicated by the summary statistics, 7-year markers were better discriminators for subgroup boys than girls.

Both sexes in the black subgroup had higher frequencies of suspect or abnormal behavior, the most important discriminator for girls, and abnormal reflexes (Table 28). A higher Bender error score was the only other marker for girls. Five of 10 discriminators for boys were unique to the subgroup: lower ratings for emotionality and self-confidence; febrile seizures; abnormal reflexes; and more younger half-siblings. The most important markers were head circumference, household moves, and family size. The canonical correlation between the discriminating characteristics at age 7 and the subgroup classification was considerably higher for boys (.26) than for girls (.12).

All Discriminators

Results of the analyses of all discriminators from the two developmental periods are shown in Table 29. Approximately three-fourths of the risk factors and 90% of the markers were retained in each subgroup. Canonical correlations were higher than those for risk factors alone as were rates of correct classification of control children. Except for sex ratio, the most important discriminators were the 7-year markers of reported mental illness and global behavior rating in the white subgroup and bilateral hearing impairment and family size in the black subgroup. Replicating results in the larger groups, both subgroups differed from controls on number of prenatal visits, sex ratio, and global behavior rating at age 7. Early discriminators eliminated from the final summary analyses were parity in both subgroups, IQ at age 4 for whites, and prior fetal death for blacks. Seven-year markers eliminated were maternal education for whites and the self-confidence rating and public assistance for blacks.

Study center differences between subgroup children and their controls were present only among whites (Table 5, Appendix 4). All discriminators in the white subgroup were reanalyzed with five centers entered. One overrepresented and one underrepresented center were retained resulting in only a few minor changes in some coefficients and no change in the canonical correlation (Table 6, Appendix 4).

All discriminators by sex in the white subgroup are shown in Table 30. As in the total group, more risk factors and fewer markers were retained for girls (85

Table 27
Sex Differences in Discriminators at Age Seven in the White Lower Achieving Subgroup

Variable	Boys				Girls			
	Mean or Percent		t or χ^2	Standardized Coefficient	Mean or Percent		t or χ^2	Standardized Coefficient
	LA Subgroup	Controls			LA Subgroup	Controls		
Self-confidence rating	2.6	2.8	3.20**	−.43	2.8	2.8	0.78	—
Housing density	1.3	1.2	4.37****	.40	1.3	1.2	2.08*	—
Fearfulness rating	2.9	3.0	2.75**	−.39	3.0	3.0	0.22	—
Activity rating	3.2	3.0	4.21****	.28	3.0	2.9	0.98	—
Socioeconomic index	44.7	54.3	4.42*****	−.28	41.6	53.4	3.63***	−.30
Draw-A-Person score	90.9	95.1	3.86***	−.28	86.9	93.8	3.99****	−.36
Maternal mental illness	17.4%	8.5%	6.79**	.27	6.3%	8.9%	0.04	—
Right-left confusion	33.6%	22.5%	6.48*	.22	26.7%	18.7%	1.34	—
Suspect or abnormal behavior rating	26.1%	13.3%	12.95***	.20	26.7%	7.8%	17.82****	.49
Tactile Finger Recognition, right	4.6	4.6	1.04	—	4.4	4.7	3.37***	−.36
Abnormal reflexes	18.2%	14.1%	1.10	—	28.9%	13.6%	7.29**	.32
Auditory-Vocal Association score	82.3	84.1	1.53	—	78.0	84.0	3.71***	−.28
Canonical correlation			.25				.20	
χ^2			102.68*****				62.95*****	
Correct group classification (N)								
LA subgroup			(111) 65.8%				(45) 57.8%	
Controls			(1469) 72.1%				(1495) 76.4%	

*$p < .05$; **$p < .01$; ***$p < .001$; ****$p < .0001$; *****$p < .00001$

Table 28
Sex Differences in Discriminators at Age Seven in the Black Lower Achieving Subgroup

Variable	Boys				Girls			
	Mean or Percent		t or χ^2	Standardized Coefficient	Mean or Percent		t or χ^2	Standardized Coefficient
	LA Subgroup	Controls			LA Subgroup	Controls		
Household moves	2.5	1.9	4.09****	.38	2.2	1.9	1.06	—
Head circumference in cm	51.1	51.6	3.38***	−.36	51.1	51.0	0.28	—
Family size	5.1	4.2	3.97****	.35	5.2	4.2	2.62**	—
Younger half-siblings	0.4	0.2	3.56***	.32	0.3	0.2	0.86	—
Attention span rating	2.9	3.0	3.28**	−.31	2.9	3.0	1.85	—
Febrile seizures	8.0%	2.5%	10.49**	.28	0.0%	2.3%	0.31	—
Emotionality rating	2.8	2.9	2.64**	−.26	2.8	2.9	0.93	—
Suspect or abnormal behavior rating	13.6%	6.0%	9.58**	.26	14.9%	4.3%	9.36**	.66
Abnormal reflexes	20.7%	12.9%	5.09*	.25	23.9%	11.4%	5.65*	.47
Self-confidence rating	2.8	2.9	2.48*	−.20	2.7	2.9	2.57**	—
Bender-Gestalt error score	8.0	7.3	2.40*	—	8.8	7.6	2.77**	.47
Canonical correlation			.26				.12	
χ^2			109.83*****				23.20****	
Correct group classification (N)								
LA subgroup			(125) 56.8%				(47) 46.8%	
Controls			(1450) 74.3%				(1646) 76.6%	

*$p < .05$; **$p < .01$; ***$p < .001$; ****$p < .0001$; *****$p < .00001$

Table 29
All Discriminators Between the Lower Achieving Subgroup and Controls

	Standardized Coefficient	
	White	Black
Mental illness in study child	.30	—
Suspect or abnormal behavior rating (7 yr.)	.30	.20
Percent male	.29	.40
Fearfulness rating (7 yr.)	−.25	—
Draw-A-Person score	−.24	—
Socioeconomic index (prenatal)	−.23	—
Self-confidence rating (7 yr.)	−.21	—
Maternal heart disease during pregnancy	.21	—
Housing density	.19	—
Prenatal visits	−.18	−.09
Inhalation anesthetics at delivery	.18	—
Activity rating (7 yr.)	.17	—
German measles	−.16	—
Tactile Finger Recognition, left	−.15	—
Right-left confusion	.14	—
Major malformations	.14	—
Retardation in siblings	.13	—
Bilateral hearing impairment	—	.29
Family size	—	.26
Abnormal language expression (3 yr.)	—	.22
Head circumference (4 yr.)	—	−.22
Abnormal reflexes	—	.22
Father employed	—	.21
Emotionality rating (7 yr.)	—	−.21
Household moves	—	.19
Attention span rating (7 yr.)	—	−.18
Cigarettes per day in pregnancy	—	.17
Febrile seizures	—	.16
Father absent	—	.16
Stanford-Binet IQ	—	−.16
Social response to mother rating (8 mo.)	—	.16
Bender-Gestalt error score	—	.12
Maternal education (7 yr.)	—	−.12
Canonical correlation	.27	.28
χ^2	228.42*	258.78*
Correct group classification (N)		
LA subgroup	(156) 62.2%	(172) 63.4%
Controls	(2964) 78.0%	(3096) 78.4%

$*p < .00001$

Table 30
Sex Differences in All Discriminators in the White Lower Achieving Subgroup

	Standardized Coefficient	
	Boys	Girls
Self-confidence rating (7 yr.)	−.36	—
Fearfulness rating (7 yr.)	−.30	—
Housing density	.30	—
Inhalation anesthetics at delivery	.28	—
Maternal education (prenatal)	−.24	—
Activity rating (7 yr.)	.24	—
Draw-A-Person score	−.22	−.20
Hypotension during pregnancy	.21	—
Maternal mental illness	.21	—
Right-left confusion	.21	—
Suspect or abnormal behavior rating (7 yr.)	.20	.31
Maternal SRA score	−.18	—
Verbal communication rating (4 yr.)	.17	—
Head circumference at 1 yr.	−.15	—
Inadequate pelvis	—	.36
Bacterial infection in 3rd trimester	—	.31
Stanford-Binet IQ	—	−.30
Positive Coombs, newborn	—	.24
Retardation in mother	—	.22
Failure to hop, right	—	.21
Failure on pegboard, left	—	.20
Socioeconomic index (prenatal)	—	−.20
Major malformations	—	.19
Prepregnant weight	—	.19
Weight gain during pregnancy	—	.18
Abnormal reflexes	—	.17
Canonical correlation	.29	.30
χ^2	140.89*	146.09*
Correct group classification (N)		
LA subgroup	(111) 70.3%	(45) 60.0%
Controls	(1469) 74.5%	(1495) 85.2%

*$p < .00001$

and 50%) than boys (67 and 89%). Canonical correlations were similar in the two sexes representing a slight increase over each preceding analysis for boys but an increase over only marker variables for girls. Subgroup classification was more accurate for boys than girls and control group classification was better for girls. Children of both sexes had a lower Draw-A-Person score at age 7 than controls and a higher frequency of suspect or abnormal behavior. The most important discriminators for boys were the ratings of self-confidence and fearfulness at age 7, housing density, and the risk factor of inhalation anesthetics at delivery. For girls, inadequate pelvis and bacterial infection in pregnancy, IQ at age 4, and suspect or abnormal behavior at age 7 were the largest discriminators. Eliminated from the summary analyses were prenatal visits and 7-year socioeconomic status for both sexes, fetal heart rate and attention span at age 4 for boys, and retarded older siblings and scores on the Tactile (right) and Auditory–Vocal Association tests for girls.

One study center was overrepresented among boys in the white subgroup but was not retained in the final summary analysis. Of the three centers entered for girls, the two overrepresented ones were retained eliminating the prenatal socioeconomic index as a discriminator (Table 7, Appendix 4). The canonical correlation and coefficients for the other variables remained essentially unchanged.

Sex differences in the black subgroup tended to parallel those for whites (Table 31). More than 80% of the risk factors and one-third of the markers (one variable) were retained for girls compared with rates of 67 and 80% for boys. Canonical correlations of .29 and .27 exceeded the one for risk factors among boys and the one for markers among girls. The correct classification rate was highest for control girls. Common discriminators were a lower Stanford–Binet IQ at age 4 and, as in the white subgroup, suspect or abnormal behavior at age 7. The family characteristics of maternal parity, number of household moves reported at age 7, and presence of younger half-siblings were the most important discriminators for subgroup boys. Febrile seizures also had a relatively large coefficient. For girls in the subgroup, maternal seizures in pregnancy and abnormal language expression at age 3 were the largest discriminators. Also important were delayed motor development at 1 year of age and the maternal factors of age at menarche, smoking in pregnancy, and length of gestation at initiation of prenatal care.

Risk factors not retained in the summary analyses were absence of the father, retarded older siblings, and number of prenatal visits for boys, and maternal education and fetal heart rate in the second stage of labor for girls. Seven-year markers eliminated were head circumference and family size for boys and the Bender score and abnormal reflexes for girls. In both sexes, study center differences between the subgroup and controls were insignificant in the univariate screen.

Table 31
Sex Differences in All Discriminators in the Black Lower Achieving Subgroup

	Standardized Coefficient	
	Boys	Girls
Household moves	.36	—
Parity	.35	—
Younger half-siblings	.34	—
Febrile seizures	.30	—
Head circumference (4 yr.)	−.27	—
Attention span rating (7 yr.)	−.27	—
Cooperation rating (4 yr.)	.26	—
Social response to mother rating (8 mo.)	.23	—
Suspect or abnormal behavior rating (7 yr.)	.22	.26
Emotionality rating (7 yr.)	−.22	—
Abnormal reflexes	.20	—
Maternal height	.19	—
Stanford-Binet IQ	−.19	−.23
Self-confidence rating (7 yr.)	−.18	—
Abnormal language expression (3 yr.)	—	.47
Seizures in pregnancy	—	.39
Age at menarche	—	−.29
Cigarettes per day in pregnancy	—	.28
Delayed motor development (1 yr.)	—	.27
Gestation at registration	—	.25
Major malformations	—	.23
Failure to copy circle	—	.22
Highest FHR in 1st stage of labor	—	−.20
Canonical correlation	.29	.27
χ^2	138.12*	129.70*
Correct group classification (N)		
LA subgroup	(125) 59.2%	(47) 53.2%
Controls	(1450) 74.3%	(1646) 88.6%

*$p < .00001$

Summary

Unique precursors and correlates of low achievement were identified in a more academically impaired subgroup of children with deficits in both reading and spelling. They included behavioral, physical, and family characteristics throughout the developmental span. Differences between the lower achieving subgroup and the larger group of low achievers were most apparent in the separate analyses by sex where between 50 and 80% of all discriminators in the final summary analyses were unique to subgroup boys and girls. For girls in each subgroup, all the unique discriminators were early risk factors. Explanatory power was not increased in the subgroup, however. Many of the canonical correlations were lower than those in the larger group of low achievers.

6 The Poorest Readers

A second subgroup of low achievers selected on the basis of academic impairment consisted of children with WRAT reading scores in the lowest decile of the distribution in the combined black and white samples. The 103 poorest readers were compared on potential risk factors and markers with an equal number of control children matched for IQ at age 7 and also for ethnicity, sex, age, socioeconomic status, and study center.[1] The mean reading scores shown in Table 32 correspond to grade ratings of Kindergarten .5 for the poorest readers and 1.6 for the controls. Three-quarters of the subgroup were male and 57% were black. The mean socioeconomic index score in the prenatal period was similar to that of all low achievers in the black sample and lower than the score for all low achievers in the white sample ($t=4.17$, $p<.0001$). Eleven of the 12 study centers were represented in the subgroup, but more than 40% of the poorest readers were contributed by the University of Oregon Medical School and the Johns Hopkins Hospital.

Methods of analysis were the same as described earlier except that the *t* test for paired samples was used to compare the subgroup and controls on quantitative variables in the univariate screen. Variables passing the screen were grouped by epoch or type and entered in the following four discriminant function analyses: gestation through 1 year of age; characteristics at age 4; psychological markers at age 7; and demographic and family markers at age 7. Results from the first two analyses were combined into a summary analysis of risk factors, and those from the second two into a summary analysis of discriminators at age 7.

---

[1] We are indebted to Jerome Kagan for the suggestion of this analysis.

Table 32
Criterion and Matching Variables for the Poorest Readers and Controls

	Mean or Percent	
WRAT reading score		
Poorest readers (N = 103)	14.9 ± 2.1	$t = 26.0, p < .00001$
Controls (N = 103)	32.6 ± 6.3	
WISC IQ	94.2 ± 3.9	
Prenatal socioeconomic index	35.4 ± 16.9	
Age in months	84.0 ± 1.5	
Sex		
Male	74.8%	
Female	25.2%	
Ethnic group		
Black	57.3%	
White	42.7%	
Study center		
University of Oregon Medical School	24.3%	
Johns Hopkins Hospital	20.4%	
Pennsylvania Hospital	12.6%	
University of Tennessee College of Medicine	9.7%	
Boston Lying-In Hospital	8.7%	
Charity Hospital, New Orleans	6.8%	
Medical College of Virginia	6.8%	
University of Minnesota Hospital	4.8%	
Providence Lying-In Hospital	3.9%	
Columbia-Presbyterian Medical Center	1.0%	
New York Medical College	1.0%	

The five independent risk factors for the poorest readers include two identified in earlier across-epoch analyses—IQ at age 4 and maternal SRA score (Table 33). All variables entered as a result of the two intermediate discriminant analyses were retained. The most important discriminators were IQ score and response to directions at age 4 and score of the mother on the nonverbal SRA intelligence test. Considered chronologically, housing density in the prenatal period was higher for the poorest readers than controls and maternal SRA score was lower. At age 4, both IQ and gross motor scores were lower for subgroup children and they were rated as less responsive to directions than controls. The risk factors had a moderate canonical correlation of .35 with the group classi-

Table 33
Early Discriminators From Gestation to Age Four in the Subgroup of Poorest Readers

Variable	Mean		t	Standardized Coefficient
	PR Subgroup	Controls		
Response to directions rating	2.8	3.0	2.55*	−.48
Stanford-Binet IQ	90.4	95.4	3.07**	−.47
Maternal SRA score	34.7	38.2	2.57*	−.45
Housing density	1.7	1.4	2.63**	.30
Gross motor score	63.7	73.6	2.36*	−.18
Canonical correlation				.35
χ^2				25.85***
Correct group classification				
PR subgroup (N = 103)				54.4%
Controls (N = 103)				71.8%

* $p < .05$
** $p < .01$
***$p < .0001$

fication. Only 54% of the poorest readers but 72% of the controls were correctly classified.

Discriminators at age 7 include three previously identified psychological variables and a unique maternal marker (Table 34). They had relatively equal weights, but those with the largest coefficients were the Bender–Gestalt and Auditory–Vocal Association scores. In addition to a lower level of performance on these tests, the poorest readers were rated as having a shorter attention span than controls. Fewer of the subgroup mothers had received additional education or training in the 7 years following delivery. The canonical correlation was similar to that for risk factors but a larger proportion of the poorest readers was correctly classified. A discriminator not retained in the summary analysis was a higher frequency of public assistance to subgroup families ($\chi^2 = 5.92$, $p < .05$).

When results from the two analyses were combined (Table 35), the risk factors of housing density and IQ at age 4 and the 7-year markers of attention span, Bender–Gestalt error score, and continued maternal education remained significant. All discriminators had a canonical correlation of .41 with the group

Table 34
Discriminators at Age Seven in the Subgroup of Poorest Readers

Variable	Mean or Percent: PR Subgroup	Mean or Percent: Controls	t or χ^2	Standardized Coefficient
Bender-Gestalt error score	8.7	7.1	3.40**	.50
Auditory-Vocal Association score	73.4	77.9	3.29**	−.48
Attention span rating	2.7	3.0	3.36**	−.41
Maternal education or training since childbirth	17.6%	31.8%	4.03*	−.40
Canonical correlation				.38
χ^2				30.93***
Correct group classification				
PR subgroup (N = 103)				66.0%
Controls (N = 103)				70.9%

* $p < .05$
** $p < .001$
*** $p < .0001$

Table 35
All Discriminators Between the Poorest Readers and Controls

	Standardized Coefficient
Stanford-Binet IQ	−.43
Attention span rating (7 yr.)	−.42
Maternal education or training since childbirth	−.40
Bender-Gestalt error score	.39
Housing density (prenatal)	.34
Canonical correlation	.41
χ^2	36.74*
Correct group classification	
PR subgroup (N = 103)	61.2%
Controls (N = 103)	71.8%

*$p < .0001$

classification, correctly assigning 61% of the poorest readers and 72% of controls.

Summary

The study approach to the subgroup of poorest readers differed from the basic design in that a tighter matching procedure was used and an equal rather than a considerably larger number of control subjects was selected. Both procedures, especially the latter one, would be expected to reduce the number of significant findings as reported. However, the extreme academic impairment of the subgroup and the simplification of design by matching for ethnicity, sex, and an index of social class were expected to produce clearer and perhaps more robust results. Major findings were that the independent risk factors and markers included social class related factors, and that the remaining group differences were in performance on cognitive or motor tasks. Although this may be seen as a reflection of the inadequacy of the socioeconomic index, it can also be viewed as evidence of a highly salient relationship between certain family characteristics and academic performance in children of average intelligence. The latter interpretation is supported by a failure to identify discriminators from other noncognitive domains.

7 The Hyperactives

All low achievers in each sample were divided into hyperactive and nonhyperactive subgroups on the basis of an activity level rating at age 7. Internal comparisons were made between the two subgroups in an attempt to identify differences in developmental patterns. Learning problems and hyperactivity have often been associated as two symptoms of an underlying "minimal" brain dysfunction (Clements, 1966; Wender, 1971). A relationship between excessive or inappropriate activity and learning in the classroom is not dependent, however, on this controversial explanatory concept. The issue addressed in this chapter was in what aspects of development do hyperactive low achievers differ from nonhyperactive ones.

The methodological difficulties in assessing activity level and in establishing a cutoff for hyperactivity are well recognized (Berler & Romanczyk, 1980; Kenny, 1980). The definition used in this study has clear limitations. Activity level was observed during the psychological assessment at age 7 and rated by the examining psychologist on a five-point scale. Low achievers who received high ratings of four or five, defined as unusually active or restless or extremely overactive and restless, were classified as hyperactive. They included 19% of the white sample (80/430) and 12% of the black sample (70/564). Those receiving an average rating of three or a lower rating that indicated reduced activity were called nonhyperactive. The two subgroups in each sample were compared on antecedents and correlates in the same sequence of analyses described earlier. Sex differences within the subgroups were not examined because of the small number of hyperactive girls.

Early Risk Factors

Discriminators between hyperactive and nonhyperactive low achievers from gestation through the preschool period are shown in Table 36. There was no overlap in the white and black samples but obstetric factors were significant in both. Among whites, the most important discriminators were birthweight of the previous child, a unique risk factor, and a fetal heart rate measure. In the prenatal period, mothers of hyperactives reported a lower birthweight for the last child and less education than mothers of nonhyperactives. During delivery, induction of labor was much less frequent, and the lowest fetal heart rate recorded in first stage of labor was higher for hyperactives than for nonhyperactives. The only postnatal discriminator was the unique one of emotionality at age 4 with hyperactives receiving the higher rating.

In the black sample, the most important discriminators were a higher frequency of hydramnios at delivery, a unique risk factor, and a higher activity level at age 4. Exposure to inhalation anesthetics at delivery was more frequent among the hyperactives, and at 8 months they were rated as less responsive to their mothers than nonhyperactives. The moderate canonical correlations were similar in the two samples. Approximately two-thirds of the children in all subgroups were correctly classified. The only discriminator not retained in the summary analyses was a higher frequency of abnormal language reception at age 3 among hyperactives in the black sample ($\chi^2 = 5.24$, $p < .05$).

Markers at Age 7

Behavioral characteristics were the major discriminators between subgroups at age 7 (Table 37). Those common to hyperactives in both samples were a global rating of suspect or abnormal behavior, to which the high activity level ratings undoubtedly contributed, and other ratings of specific behaviors indicating higher impulsivity, a shorter attention span, and more assertiveness (a lower score) than in the nonhyperactive subgroups. Behavioral markers confined to only one sample were better rapport (or less shyness) with the examiner and a higher degree of dependency among white hyperactives and more emotional responsiveness, less fearfulness, and poorer goal orientation among black hyperactives. The remaining discriminators were of lesser importance. White hyperactives had a higher frequency of abnormal reflexes and a higher Bender error score than the comparison subgroup. Black hyperactives had a higher frequency of abnormal gait and a lower spelling score. Both were unique markers but spelling and the other Wide Range Achievement subtests were screened only in this subgroup and the ones defined by IQ level presented in the following chapter. The impulsivity and dependency ratings were also markers unique to hyperactives.

Discriminators at age 7 had moderately high canonical correlations of .56 and .61 with the subgroup classification in the white and black samples. About

Table 36
Early Discriminators from Gestation to Age Four in the Hyperactive Subgroup

Variable	White				Black			
	Mean or Percent		t or χ^2	Standardized Coefficient	Mean or Percent		t or χ^2	Standardized Coefficient
	Hyper-actives	Non-Hyper-actives			Hyper-actives	Non-Hyper-actives		
Birthweight of last child (g)	3086	3297	2.25*	−.49	3044	3024	0.20	—
Lowest FHR in 1st stage of labor	129.8	126.2	2.11*	.47	131.4	131.2	0.07	—
Induction of labor	1.3%	12.2%	6.98**	−.43	7.1%	5.7%	0.05	—
Emotionality rating	3.2	3.0	2.52*	.41	3.1	2.9	2.11*	—
Maternal education (yr.)	9.6	10.2	2.33*	−.39	10.3	10.0	1.18	—
Hydramnios at delivery	0.0%	1.1%	0.05	—	6.4%	0.4%	7.39**	.64
Activity rating	3.3	3.1	1.99*	—	3.3	3.0	4.19***	.59
Inhalation anesthetics at delivery	36.3%	43.5%	1.11	—	54.3%	41.0%	3.90*	.38
Social response to mother rating (8 mo.)	3.3	3.2	1.15	—	3.1	3.3	2.29*	−.32
Canonical correlation		.28				.31		
χ^2		34.86****				56.31****		
Correct group classification (N)								
Hyperactives		(80) 60.0%				(70) 64.3%		
Non-Hyperactives		(349) 65.0%				(494) 65.4%		

$^*p < .05$; $^{**}p < .01$; $^{***}p < .0001$; $^{****}p < .00001$

Table 37
Discriminators at Age Seven in the Hyperactive Subgroup

Variable	White				Black			
	Mean or Percent		t or χ^2	Standardized Coefficient	Mean or Percent		t or χ^2	Standardized Coefficient
	Hyper-actives	Non-Hyper-actives			Hyper-actives	Non-Hyper-actives		
Impulsivity rating	3.3	2.9	6.66****	.38	3.4	3.0	9.79****	.27
Suspect or abnormal behavior rating	46.3%	16.9%	30.60****	.34	47.1%	7.5%	85.07****	.41
Attention span rating	2.5	2.9	7.31****	−.31	2.5	3.0	8.71****	−.22
Rapport with examiner rating	3.3	2.9	5.61****	.28	3.4	2.9	5.99****	—
Assertiveness rating	2.8	3.2	6.56****	−.25	2.8	3.3	7.81****	−.16
Dependency rating	3.4	3.2	4.37***	.21	3.3	3.1	5.03****	—
Abnormal reflexes	31.7%	15.5%	10.06*	.18	17.6%	14.5%	0.26	—
Bender-Gestalt error score	8.3	6.9	3.47**	.15	8.4	8.4	0.03	—
Emotionality rating	3.3	2.9	5.91****	—	3.2	2.8	7.02****	.22
Fearfulness rating	2.7	3.0	4.24***	—	2.5	3.0	6.07****	−.21
Abnormal gait	6.3%	4.9%	0.06	—	7.4%	1.5%	7.04*	.21
Goal orientation rating	2.6	2.8	3.81**	—	2.7	3.0	6.82****	−.18
WRAT spelling score	19.7	20.0	0.94	—	18.5	20.0	3.68**	−.13
Canonical correlation			.56				.61	
χ^2			156.35****				254.20****	
Correct group classification (N)								
Hyperactives			(80) 66.3%				(70) 65.7%	
Non-Hyperactives			(349) 87.4%				(494) 93.5%	

*$p < .01$; **$p < .001$; ***$p < .0001$; ****$p < .00001$

two-thirds of the hyperactives and 90% of the nonhyperactives were correctly classified. Not retained in the summary analyses were ratings of more emotional responsiveness (Table 37) and less anxiety when separated from the caretaker ($t = 2.64$, $p < .05$) among white hyperactives and higher frequencies of impaired extraocular movements ($\chi^2 = 5.87$, $p < .05$) and right–left confusion ($\chi^2 = 6.57$, $p < .05$) among black hyperactives.

All Discriminators

The results of combining all discriminators in a single analysis are shown in Table 38. For hyperactives in the white sample, the markers of suspect or abnormal behavior and impulsivity had the highest coefficients. The obstetric characteristics of fewer induced labors and a higher fetal heart rate measure

Table 38
All Discriminators Between the Hyperactive and Non-Hyperactive Subgroups

	Standardized Coefficient	
	White	Black
Impulsivity rating (7 yr.)	.36	.28
Suspect or abnormal behavior rating (7 yr.)	.36	.41
Attention span rating (7 yr.)	−.30	−.17
Rapport with examiner rating (7 yr.)	.28	—
Assertiveness rating (7 yr.)	−.24	−.16
Dependency rating (7 yr.)	.20	—
Induction of labor	−.18	—
Lowest FHR in 1st stage of labor	.18	—
Abnormal reflexes	.17	—
Hydramnios at delivery	—	.34
Fearfulness rating (7 yr.)	—	−.21
Goal orientation rating (7 yr.)	—	−.21
Abnormal gait	—	.20
Emotionality rating (7 yr.)	—	.18
Inhalation anesthetics at delivery	—	.12
Canonical correlation	.57	.64
χ^2	165.46*	295.71*
Correct group classification (N)		
Hyperactives	(80) 67.5%	(70) 70.0%
Non-Hyperactives	(349) 87.4%	(494) 94.5%

*$p < .00001$

were retained from the early developmental period. All the markers entered were significant with the exception of the Bender–Gestalt score. In the black sample, the global rating of suspect or abnormal behavior at age 7 and the risk factor of hydramnios at delivery were the most important discriminators between hyperactive and nonhyperactive low achievers. The other significant risk factor was inhalation anesthetics at delivery. The WRAT spelling score was the only marker not retained in the analysis. The moderately high canonical correlations in both samples and the rates of correct classification were similar to those for discriminators at age 7.

One study center was overrepresented among hyperactives in each sample and was entered and subsequently retained in the final summary analysis (Table 8, Appendix 4). There was little effect on the canonical correlations and no change in discriminators in the black sample. Among whites, however, fetal heart rate and abnormal reflexes, discriminators with relatively low coefficients, were eliminated and the emotionality rating at age 4 and the Bender score, also with low coefficients, were added to the analysis.

Summary

Extreme ratings on an activity level scale were used to identify a subgroup of hyperactive low achievers who were then compared on developmental indices with the nonhyperactive low achievers. Although this was an internal comparison not involving a control group, it is of some importance to note that the proportion of hyperactives among the low achievers was significantly higher than among their academically successful controls (19 versus 10% and 12 versus 8% in the white and black samples, respectively). The subgroups differed from each other primarily on other behavioral indices with the hyperactives characterized in general as non-normal in behavior and specifically as more labile and less task oriented than nonhyperactives. Two robust risk factors for hyperactivity, however, were identified in the black sample. They were the obstetric factors of hydramnios or excess amniotic fluid at delivery and the use of inhalation anesthetics.

8 The IQ Subgroups

A second internal comparison was made among subgroups of low achievers at different IQ levels. Children with relatively high IQ scores at age 7 were of primary interest because of the larger aptitude–achievement discrepancy in this subgroup. The overestimation of intellectual ability among the learning disabled has been described by Feagans (1983) as conventional folklore that is in contrast to the findings that learning-disabled children as a group score lower than normal children on intelligence tests. Owen et al. (1971) found that a relatively high IQ subgroup of middle-class educationally handicapped children was characterized by signs of personality maladjustment and the absence of physiological–organic impairment and language problems. Rie (1980) has suggested that psychogenic determinants must be considered for bright children with learning and/or behavioral disabilities, whereas for the lower IQ children more "organicity" is to be expected.

A less than optimal definition of the IQ subgroups was dictated by the narrow range of WISC Full Scale scores among the low achievers and the relatively few high IQs. The ranges selected for the low, medium, and high subgroups were 90–94, 95–104, and 105–128, respectively. Mean IQ scores in the three subgroups were 92 ± 1.3, 99 ± 2.8, and 111 ± 4.7 in the white sample and 92 ± 1.4, 98 ± 2.7, and 109 ± 3.4 in the black sample. The proportion of low achievers in the low and high subgroups was 43 and 15% in the white sample and 51 and 7% in the black sample. In the initial screening of antecedents and correlates, comparisons were made among the three IQ subgroups. Variables that were significant ($p < .05$) were categorized by epoch or type and entered in three–group discriminant function analyses in the previously described sequence.

Early Risk Factors

Discriminators among IQ subgroups in the white sample from gestation through age 4 are shown in Table 39. The most important was the earlier IQ score at age 4 that increased linearly across subgroups from a mean of 92 to 101. Height at age 4 and the gross motor score also discriminated among subgroups with shorter stature and poorer motor performance in the low IQ subgroup. In the prenatal period, the pregnancy complications of vaginal bleeding, a relatively low hemoglobin, and bleeding at admission for delivery were more frequent in the low IQ subgroup. Bleeding in pregnancy was also more frequent in the medium than the high IQ subgroup. Maternal height and nonverbal intelligence test score (SRA) were higher in the high IQ subgroup and the frequency of employment in the prenatal period was greater. Postnatal discriminators in addition to the characteristics at age 4 were sex of child with a higher proportion of males in the high IQ subgroup and a behavior rating at 8 months indicating a more intense social response in this subgroup.

All discriminators had a moderately high canonical correlation of .45 with the subgroup classification. Correct classification rates ranged from 32% in the medium IQ subgroup to 61% in the high subgroup.

IQ at age 4 was also the most important discriminator among subgroups in the black sample (Table 40). The other common discriminator was the maternal nonverbal intelligence test score. The earlier IQ of the low achievers and the maternal score were highest in the high IQ subgroup. In the prenatal and perinatal periods, reports of a prior fetal death were more frequent among mothers of the high IQ children and there were more induced labors in this subgroup. The Apgar score at 1 minute was relatively low in the medium IQ subgroup. Postnatal discriminators other than IQ at age 4 were a shorter duration of response to objects at 8 months in the low IQ subgroup, and a higher fine motor score at age 4 in the high IQ subgroup.

The moderate canonical correlation of .37 between all early discriminators and the subgroup classification was somewhat lower than in the white sample. Correct classification rates were similar with the highest accuracy in the high IQ subgroup and the lowest in the medium subgroup.

Markers at Age 7

The Auditory–Vocal Association Test and the WRAT Arithmetic subtest were the major discriminators among IQ subgroups in both samples (Tables 41 and 42). Each test score increased linearly with IQ level. The other marker common to both samples was the Draw-A-Person test with lower scores in the low IQ subgroups. Among whites, the Bender–Gestalt error score was higher among children in the low IQ subgroup and they were rated as more likely to withdraw from a frustrating task. The high IQ subgroup was rated as the most self-confident. Level of maternal education was higher in the high IQ subgroup,

Table 39
Early Discriminators from Gestation to Age Four Among the White IQ Subgroups

Variable	Mean or Percent: Low IQ	Medium IQ	High IQ		t or χ^2	Standardized Coefficient
Stanford-Binet IQ (4 yr.)	92.0	97.1	101.1	LM	4.06***	.55
				LH	4.86****	
				MH	2.49*	
Height in cm (4 yr.)	99.6	100.8	100.9	LM	2.09*	.37
Lowest hemoglobin in pregnancy	10.8	11.1	11.3	LM	2.12*	.31
				LH	2.36*	
Vaginal bleeding in pregnancy	49.1%	44.1%	25.0%	LH	9.63**	.31
				MH	6.03*	
Vaginal bleeding at admission for delivery	12.0%	4.5%	3.1%	LM	5.83*	.28
Mother employed	3.9%	8.9%	14.1%	LH	6.40*	.24
Percent male	63.0%	69.2%	85.9%	LH	10.58**	.24
				MH	5.97*	
Intensity of social response rating (8 mo.)	3.0	3.0	3.2	LH	2.64**	.21
				MH	2.21*	
Gross motor score	63.4	71.1	66.3	LM	2.72**	.19
Maternal height (in.)	63.4	63.0	64.0	MH	2.59**	.17
Maternal SRA score	39.2	39.0	42.9	LH	2.68**	.04
				MH	2.64**	
Canonical correlation						.45
χ^2						132.79****
Correct group classification						
Low IQ (N = 184)						56.5%
Medium IQ (N = 182)						32.4%
High IQ (N = 64)						60.9%

Note — LM, LH, and MH identify univariate comparisons between the low-medium, low-high, and medium-high IQ subgroups, respectively.
$*p < .05$; $**p < .01$; $***p < .0001$; $****p < .00001$

Table 40
Early Discriminators from Gestation to Age Four Among the Black IQ Subgroups

Variable	Mean or Percent Low IQ	Medium IQ	High IQ		t or χ^2	Standardized Coefficient
Stanford-Binet IQ (4 yr.)	89.9	93.1	104.1	LM LH MH	2.93** 6.87**** 5.43****	.66
Fine motor score	71.0	71.3	83.6	LH MH	4.03*** 4.18***	.34
Induction of labor	5.5%	4.6%	15.0%	MH	4.68*	.31
Maternal SRA score	33.4	34.8	38.3	LH	2.26*	.25
Prior fetal death	13.9%	12.3%	28.6%	MH	4.82*	.19
Apgar score (1 min.)	8.1	7.7	8.5	LM MH	2.12* 2.37*	.15
Duration of response rating (8 mo.)	3.1	3.2	3.4	LM LH	2.51* 2.81**	.12
Canonical correlation						.37
χ^2						105.52****
Correct group classification						
Low IQ (N = 286)						53.5%
Medium IQ (N = 236)						33.1%
High IQ (N = 42)						64.3%

*$p < .05$; **$p < .01$; ***$p < .0001$; ****$p < .00001$

housing density was low, and multiple pregnancies in the family, a unique 7-year discriminator, were more frequent. The only pediatric marker was head circumference, which was slightly larger in the high IQ subgroup.

In the black sample, an additional psychological discriminator was a rating of rapport with the examiner that increased across IQ subgroups. The socioeconomic index score at age 7 was lowest in the low IQ subgroup. Reported mental illness in siblings was most frequent in the high IQ subgroup. With the exception of weight at age 7, which increased with IQ level, pediatric markers were not indicative of any consistent subgroup differences. Surgery was performed more frequently in the medium IQ subgroup and mumps was

Table 41
Discriminators at Age Seven Among the White IQ Subgroups

Variable	Mean or Percent			t or χ^2		Standardized Coefficient
	Low IQ	Medium IQ	High IQ			
Auditory-Vocal Association score	77.7	81.7	87.5	LM	3.79***	.42
				LH	6.32*****	
				MH	3.84***	
WRAT arithmetic score	18.3	19.5	20.6	LM	4.03****	.36
				LH	5.25*****	
				MH	2.54*	
Bender-Gestalt error score	8.1	6.7	5.9	LM	4.49*****	.29
				LH	4.81*****	
Draw-A-Person score	87.3	92.2	93.8	LM	4.13****	.27
				LH	4.34****	
Head circumference (cm)	51.1	51.2	51.8	LH	3.26**	.24
				MH	2.65**	
Maternal education (yr.)	9.9	10.1	11.3	LH	4.06****	.22
				MH	3.47***	
Frustration tolerance rating	2.7	2.8	2.9	LM	2.76**	.17
				LH	2.89**	
Self-confidence rating	2.6	2.6	2.8	LH	2.01*	.10
				MH	2.48*	
Subsequent multiple pregnancies	4.6%	0.9%	13.2%	MH	7.88**	.09
Housing density	1.3	1.3	1.1	LH	2.88**	.05
				MH	3.22**	
Canonical correlation						.48
χ^2						149.57*****
Correct group classification						
Low IQ (N = 184)						62.0%
Medium IQ (N = 182)						28.0%
High IQ (N = 64)						70.3%

*$p < .05$; **$p < .01$; ***$p < .001$; ****$p < .0001$; *****$p < .00001$

Table 42
Discriminators at Age Seven Among the Black IQ Subgroups

Variable	Mean or Percent				t or χ^2	Standardized Coefficient
	Low IQ	Medium IQ	High IQ			
Auditory-Vocal Association score	71.8	74.5	85.6	LM	3.05**	.56
				LH	8.33*****	
				MH	6.48*****	
WRAT arithmetic score	18.4	19.4	21.6	LM	3.65***	.35
				LH	6.44*****	
				MH	4.78*****	
Rapport with examiner rating	2.8	3.0	3.3	LM	2.07*	.32
				LH	4.02****	
				MH	2.84**	
Draw-A-Person score	91.8	94.7	95.6	LM	2.74**	.21
Socioeconomic index	34.4	38.0	43.9	LM	2.09*	.21
				LH	3.01**	
Weight (kg)	23.2	24.1	25.8	LM	2.60**	.19
				LH	4.02****	
				MH	2.17*	
Mental illness in siblings	2.2%	1.1%	9.1%	MH	4.47*	.18
Café au lait spots	4.0%	0.4%	2.4%	LM	5.50*	.15
Mumps	14.3%	10.0%	24.4%	MH	5.52*	.09
Surgery	11.4%	19.1%	9.8%	LM	5.25*	.07
Canonical correlation						.45
χ^2						154.14*****
Correct group classification						
Low IQ (N = 286)						62.2%
Medium IQ (N = 236)						41.1%
High IQ (N = 42)						73.8%

*$p < .05$; **$p < .01$; ***$p < .001$; ****$p < .0001$; *****$p < .00001$

reported more often in the high subgroup. Café au lait spots, a minor skin malformation, were more frequent in the low IQ subgroup.

Canonical correlations between markers and the subgroup classification were moderate and, in the black sample, slightly higher than the one for early discriminators. Correct classification rates were approximately 70% in the high IQ subgroups, 60% in the low subgroups, and 30 to 40% in the medium subgroups.

All Discriminators

Independent differences among IQ subgroups in the early and late periods combined are shown in Table 43. In the white sample, the most important discriminators were performance on the Auditory–Vocal Association and WRAT Arithmetic tests at age 7. From the 11 early discriminators entered, the four retained were vaginal bleeding in pregnancy, maternal SRA score, social response at 8 months, and gross motor score at age 4. All the markers except for the two demographic ones of maternal education and housing density remained significant. The canonical correlation between all discriminators and the subgroup classification in the white sample was .51 with correct classification rates of 66 and 61% in the high and low IQ subgroups and 38% in the medium subgroup.

In the black sample, the Auditory–Vocal Association score and the WRAT Arithmetic score were the first and third ranked discriminators among IQ subgroups and were the only variables significant in both samples. Second in importance was the IQ score at age 4. In contrast to the white sample, six of seven early discriminators were retained. The exception was the maternal SRA score. Markers no longer significant were the Draw-A-Person score, weight, and the socioeconomic index. All discriminators had a canonical correlation of .49 with the subgroup classification, correctly classifying 74% of the high IQ subgroup, 55% of the low subgroup, and 45% of those with IQs in the medium range.

Study centers that were unequally represented among the IQ subgroups were entered in the analyses of all discriminators. One center was overrepresented in the high IQ subgroup in both samples, and, among blacks, a center was overrepresented in the medium IQ subgroup and another was underrepresented. All were retained in the final summary analyses producing no change in the other discriminators and only negligible effects on the canonical correlations (Table 9, Appendix 4). There were some shifts in the correct classification rates with increased accuracy in the medium IQ subgroups.

Summary

Developmental differences among subgroups of low achievers at three IQ levels were examined. Although the range of WISC Full Scale scores at age 7

Table 43
All Discriminators Among IQ Subgroups

	Standardized Coefficient	
	White	Black
Auditory-Vocal Association score	.43	.37
WRAT arithmetic score	.34	.31
Intensity of social response rating (8 mo.)	.27	—
Vaginal bleeding in pregnancy	.26	—
Head circumference (7 yr.)	.25	—
Draw-A-Person score	.25	—
Bender-Gestalt error score	.25	—
Self-confidence rating (7 yr.)	.14	—
Frustration tolerance rating (7 yr.)	.11	—
Maternal SRA score	.11	—
Subsequent multiple pregnancies	.09	—
Gross motor score	.04	—
Stanford-Binet IQ	—	.35
Rapport with examiner rating (7 yr.)	—	.30
Fine motor score	—	.25
Mental illness in siblings	—	.21
Induction of labor	—	.15
Café au lait spots	—	.14
Prior fetal death	—	.11
Mumps	—	.11
Duration of response rating (8 mo.)	—	.10
Surgery	—	.05
Apgar score (1 min.)	—	.03
Canonical correlation	.51	.49
χ^2	178.07*	204.26*
Correct group classification (N)		
Low IQ	(184) 61.4%	(286) 55.2%
Medium IQ	(182) 38.5%	(236) 45.3%
High IQ	(64) 65.6%	(42) 73.8%

$*p < .00001$

was narrow, consistent differences were found between subgroups with relatively high and relatively low IQs. A medium IQ subgroup was less well characterized. Not unexpectedly, the high IQ subgroup in both samples had relatively high verbal, perceptual–motor, and numerical skills and showed more adaptive behavior in the testing situation. Maternal aptitude scores were highest in this subgroup in both samples. Noncognitive factors associated with a higher IQ level were indices of larger physical size and higher socioeconomic status. The more unexpected findings that could be risk factors for this subgroup of low achievers were a very high male to female ratio among whites and higher frequencies of prior fetal death, induced labor, and reported mental illness in siblings among blacks. Characteristics of the low IQ subgroups were, in general, the opposite of those of the high subgroups. In addition, pregnancy complications including bleeding were more frequent in this subgroup in the white sample.

9 Summary and Discussion

This was a study of the characteristics of young children with unexpectedly low academic achievement, unexpected because of their normal aptitude or intelligence. The sample consisted of 7-year-old white and black children in the first and second grades who had been followed since gestation in the Collaborative Perinatal Project. Both maturational and environmental antecedents and correlates of low achievement were investigated. The sample could well have been called learning disabled although it was selected from a nonclinic or nonreferred population on the basis of a discrepancy between IQ and achievement test scores. The controversy surrounding learning disabilities involves the basic issues of definition, a problem that has practical as well as theoretical implications and the relative importance of endogenous and exogenous determinants. The general findings of this study of low achievement were that a broad array of prospectively determined physical, social, and behavioral characteristics had only moderate explanatory power, and that exogenous or environmental factors were more highly related to low achievement than endogenous ones.

Specific descriptive findings were that approximately 3% of children in the Collaborative Perinatal Project population were low achievers, a proportion at the lower limit of most prevalence estimates of learning disabilities. Over two-thirds of the group were boys in both the white and black samples. Mean WISC IQ scores, required by sample selection criteria to be at least 90, were 98 and 96 for whites and blacks, respectively. Low achievers had lower scores than IQ-matched controls on the WISC subtests of Digit Span, Information, and among blacks, Picture Arrangement. Their WRAT grade ratings in arithmetic, as well as in the criterion areas of reading and spelling, were lower than those of controls.

Low achievers were required to have low grade ratings in either reading or spelling on the Wide Range Achievement Test. In a lower achieving subgroup with deficits in both areas (approximately one-third of the original group), unique predictors and correlates were identified in several areas, but their explanatory power was no greater than those in the larger group. There were marked sex differences in the white and black subgroups. Early risk factors were better discriminators for girls than boys.

A subgroup of poor readers with reading scores in the lowest decile of the distribution was compared with controls matched not only on IQ but on socioeconomic status, ethnic group, sex, and institution or study center. Their mean reading score corresponded to a grade rating of Kindergarten .5. Independent discriminators from both the early and late periods included the social class related factors of maternal intelligence, maternal education, and housing density, and indices of cognitive and motor development.

In two comparisons within the group of low achievers, those rated as hyperactive were compared with the nonhyperactives, and low achievers at three IQ levels were compared. The hyperactives were characterized mainly by non-normal behavior in other areas, specifically emotional lability, and lack of task orientation. In the black sample, hydramnios at delivery and use of inhalation anesthetics were also related to hyperactivity. The relatively high IQ group had better cognitive skills, and their mothers had higher nonverbal intelligence test scores and higher socioeconomic status. Among whites, there was a very large excess of males, and among blacks, reported mental illness in siblings.

Major findings in this study support and augment the conclusions of others that lower socioeconomic status, less maternal education, higher birth order, and larger family size are related to higher rates of academic failure (Alberman, 1973; Bell et al., 1976, 1977; Belmont et al., 1976; Davie et al., 1972; Kappelman et al., 1972; Ramey et al., 1978; Werner, 1980). Sex of child as a predictor of learning disabilities is consistent with many epidemiological reports of the preponderance of boys in this category (Belmont, 1980; Maccoby & Jacklin, 1974; Norman & Zigmond, 1980). Sex differences in antecedents and correlates of low achievement were identified in both ethnic groups. That these results often differed in the two samples is perhaps not surprising, because sex differences are generally viewed as complex, multidetermined outcomes of interaction between environmental and biological processes (Eme, 1979). Low achievement in boys was primarily related to aspects of the caretaking environment, a finding in agreement with others reporting a greater vulnerability of male children to family disruption (Hoffman, 1979; Rutter, 1970). Boys in the white sample had early speech production or intelligibility problems, a predictor identified by Lyle (1970), and girls in the black sample had early expressive language problems, a more severe developmental language disorder (Bishop, 1979). The lower preschool IQ of white girls and the lower 7-year Verbal IQ of girls in both samples tend to support the hypothesis that girls with learning problems are more intellectually handicapped than boys (Owen, 1978).

Although a more academically impaired subgroup of low achievers was less homogeneous than expected, behavioral problems were found to be prominant among whites and physical problems among blacks. The association between poor academic performance and behavioral maladjustment is well recognized (Boder, 1976; Davie et al., 1972; Kohn, 1977; Rutter, Tizard, Yule, Graham, & Whitmore, 1976), although the direction of the relationship is not always agreed upon. Problems in either the academic or behavioral areas may be primary in different groups of children, or both symptoms may have a common etiology. The suspicious neurological findings and definite sensory abnormality in the black subgroup are indicative of a relationship between learning problems and clinical signs of central nervous system impairment evident on physical examination (Adams, Kocsis, & Estes, 1974; Barlow, 1974; Clements, 1966; Hughes, 1978). The hearing deficit in this subgroup affected only 1% of the children and was the only definite sensory or neurological abnormality identified in the study sample. The rarity of such conditions among academically handicapped children was reported by Owen et al. (1971). In agreement with findings of Belmont and Birch (1965), right–left confusion was a consistent discriminator in both the total group and the subgroup among whites.

Pregnancy and perinatal complications were important discriminators for girls in the lower achieving subgroup, and to a lesser extent, for white boys. Factors significant in the final summary analyses were the pregnancy complications of bacterial infection, maternal seizures, hypotension, and cigarette smoking; the delivery conditions of inadequate pelvis, lower fetal heart rate, and use of inhalation anesthetic agents; and the newborn complications of malformations and Rh sensitivity. Longer labor and toxemia, predictors of learning problems in other studies (Kappelman et al., 1972; Kawi & Pasamanick, 1959) were consistently significant in the larger group of low achievers in the black sample but not in the subgroup. Perinatal factors have also been associated with hyperactivity in children (Pasamanick, Rodgers, & Lilienfeld, 1956; Ross & Ross, 1976). In this study, lower birthweight in older siblings, hydramnios at delivery, and use of inhalation anesthetics were among the best predictors of hyperactivity in low achievers.

The performance levels of low achievers were lower than those of their IQ-matched controls in psychomotor, verbal, and tactile–perceptual areas. Similar deficits in children with learning problems have been reported by others (Elkins & Sultmann, 1981; Finlayson & Reitan, 1976; Owen et al., 1971). Within the low achieving group, performance levels were directly related to IQ. Those with relatively high IQs had not only the highest IQs at age 4 but also the highest scores on tests of psychomotor and verbal ability at age 7. They were also larger, of higher socioeconomic status, and had a lower frequency of perinatal complications than children with lower IQs.

With the exception of the contribution of genetic factors, not investigated because of the small number of siblings or cousins meeting the definitional criteria, most of the etiological theories of learning disabilities were explored in this study. Although low achievers differed from controls in several areas of development, the importance of sociocultural factors as discriminators lends indirect support to the hypothesis of a primary verbal deficit (Vellutino, 1977). Those aspects of the family environment associated with low achievement are also the ones associated with opportunities for verbal–conceptual learning. The lower socioeconomic status, larger family size, and higher birth order of low achievers could all have contributed to the restriction of these opportunities, resulting in poor verbal skills that were detectable in the preschool period. Less parental press for academic achievement has also been associated with lower socioeconomic status (Schaefer, 1984). Although biological factors were identified as antecedents and correlates of low achievement, they were diffuse and relatively weak as discriminators. An important implication of the verbal deficit hypothesis is that diagnostic and remedial techniques should focus directly on the skills that need to be acquired (Vellutino et al., 1977).

Children with deficits in reading or other basic academic areas may not remain at the end of the continuum (Belmont & Belmont, 1978), and it would have been desirable to follow up the children in this study who were only 7 years of age. Promising designs for future studies, both cross sectional and longitudinal, will undoubtedly include new techniques for the investigation of neurophysiological processes associated with learning and learning disabilities.

Appendix 1

DESCRIPTIVE STATISTICS FOR LOW ACHIEVERS AND CONTROLS BY ETHNIC GROUP

The table in this appendix contains all variables that passed the univariate screen in the initial comparison between low achievers and controls. Means, standard deviations, frequencies (complete data counts), and measures of skewness are presented for each variable for low achievers and controls in the two ethnic groups. These data permit the reader to exercise his or her own judgment, possibly using criteria other than those employed in this study, regarding the level of statistical significance and the potential ramifications of deviations from underlying statistical assumptions.

Table 1
Descriptive Statistics for Variables Passing the Univariate Screen for Low Achievers and Controls by Ethnic Group

Variable and Group	White				Black			
	Mean	S.D.	N	Skewness	Mean	S.D.	N	Skewness
Prenatal Family and Maternal								
1. Socioeconomic index								
Low achievers	43.42	17.63	421	0.53	36.14	16.44	552	0.34
Controls	53.90	19.81	2505	0.04	40.27	17.58	3288	0.34
2. Housing density								
Low achievers	1.25	0.67	422	4.27	1.66	0.90	553	2.36
Controls	1.13	0.50	2501	1.90	1.53	0.83	3319	2.14
3. Father absent								
Low achievers	0.18	0.38	423	−1.68	0.39	0.49	557	−0.44
Controls	0.13	0.34	2526	−2.21	0.34	0.47	3329	−0.68
4. Retarded siblings								
Low achievers	0.06	0.24	313	3.70	0.06	0.24	337	3.64
Controls	0.04	0.20	1649	4.66 NS	0.04	0.19	1968	4.94
5. Maternal education (yr.)								
Low achievers	10.13	2.19	423	−0.23	10.04	2.03	555	−0.75
Controls	10.93	2.25	2512	−0.44	10.52	1.92	3333	−0.73
6. Maternal SRA score								
Low achievers	39.57	7.76	274	−1.21	34.31	8.21	298	−0.63
Controls	40.83	7.16	1672	−0.82	34.70	8.06	1988	−0.66 NS
7. Mother employed								
Low achievers	0.08	0.27	423	3.22	0.12	0.33	557	2.29
Controls	0.15	0.35	2525	2.02	0.14	0.35	3332	2.04 NS
8. Parity								
Low achievers	2.44	2.00	430	0.97	2.64	2.51	564	1.05
Controls	1.85	1.97	2572	1.52	2.15	2.19	3379	1.32
9. Length of pregnancy-free interval (yr.)								
Low achievers	1.74	2.06	351	3.83	1.69	2.14	425	3.34
Controls	1.76	2.00	1817	2.90 NS	1.94	2.38	2451	2.97

(continued)

Table 1 (continued)

Variable and Group	White				Black			
	Mean	S.D.	N	Skewness	Mean	S.D.	N	Skewness
Prenatal Family and Maternal								
10. Prepregnant weight (lb.)								
Low achievers	131.84	30.05	427	1.47	135.67	29.86	543	1.81
Controls	128.79	23.79	2514	1.49	133.67	27.64	3304	1.47[NS]
11. Cigarette smoking history (yr.)								
Low achievers	5.71	5.68	426	0.97	3.65	4.96	558	1.70
Controls	5.12	5.39	2541	1.18	3.43	4.99	3316	1.79[NS]
Pregnancy and Perinatal								
12. Gestation at registration (wk.)								
Low achievers	22.82	8.78	430	0.22	23.44	7.30	564	0.09
Controls	20.84	9.04	2578	0.42	22.61	7.33	3379	0.15
13. Number of hospitalizations since LMP								
Low achievers	0.25	0.70	427	4.22	0.16	0.43	560	2.82
Controls	0.18	0.51	2561	3.49	0.18	0.48	3354	3.90[NS]
14. Cigarettes per day in pregnancy								
Low achievers	10.16	11.81	430	1.20	4.17	6.72	562	1.73
Controls	9.00	10.90	2557	1.14	3.66	6.82	3361	2.63[NS]
15. Edema during pregnancy								
Low achievers	0.49	0.50	412	0.06	0.24	0.43	535	1.24
Controls	0.42	0.49	2456	0.31	0.25	0.43	3236	1.16[NS]
16. Maternal heart disease during pregnancy								
Low achievers	0.03	0.17	425	5.47	0.01	0.12	556	8.18
Controls	0.02	0.12	2558	8.03	0.02	0.13	3339	7.75[NS]
17. Toxemia during pregnancy								
Low achievers	0.09	0.28	368	2.94	0.12	0.32	511	2.38
Controls	0.10	0.30	2217	2.71[NS]	0.09	0.28	3054	2.96

(continued)

Table 1 (continued)

Variable and Group	White				Black			
	Mean	S.D.	N	Skewness	Mean	S.D.	N	Skewness
Pregnancy and Perinatal								
18. Number of prenatal visits								
Low achievers	8.54	4.18	430	0.34	7.40	3.44	564	0.28
Controls	9.81	4.21	2578	0.14	8.19	3.70	3380	0.44
19. Inhalation anesthetics at delivery								
Low achievers	0.42	0.49	426	0.33	0.43	0.50	558	0.30
Controls	0.29	0.46	2561	0.90	0.44	0.50	3356	0.24 NS
20. Length of 1st stage of labor (hr.)								
Low achievers	6.87	5.57	382	2.42	8.19	6.13	430	1.60
Controls	7.29	4.91	2329	1.60 NS	7.39	5.46	2525	1.86
21. Forceps delivery								
Low achievers	0.46	0.50	380	0.17	0.27	0.45	513	1.02
Controls	0.57	0.50	2324	−0.27	0.30	0.46	3054	0.87 NS
22. Gestational age (wk.)								
Low achievers	39.94	2.91	427	−0.05	38.76	3.42	554	−0.55
Controls	39.98	2.41	2573	−0.47 NS	39.06	3.01	3338	−0.55
23. Sex of child (% male)								
Low achievers	0.69	0.46	430	0.83	0.67	0.47	564	0.74
Controls	0.49	0.50	2580	−0.02	0.46	0.50	3384	−0.16
24. Apgar score at 1 min.								
Low achievers	7.39	2.09	397	−1.38	7.94	1.93	499	−1.71
Controls	7.66	1.90	2422	−1.62	7.97	1.88	3086	−1.70 NS
25. Apgar score at 5 min.								
Low achievers	8.74	1.11	403	−2.69	9.09	1.22	515	−3.05
Controls	8.89	1.00	2456	−3.39	9.10	1.23	3168	−3.03 NS
26. Respiratory difficulty in newborn								
Low achievers	0.03	0.18	425	5.25	0.02	0.14	563	6.96
Controls	0.02	0.12	2559	7.92	0.02	0.12	3368	8.03 NS

(continued)

Table 1 (continued)

Variable and Group	White				Black			
	Mean	S.D.	N	Skewness	Mean	S.D.	N	Skewness
Infancy								
27. Bayley Motor Scale score at 8 mo.								
Low achievers	32.68	4.95	320	−0.65	33.20	4.58	460	−0.95
Controls	33.02	4.44	2106	−0.58[NS]	33.62	4.07	2836	−0.55
28. Intensity of social response rating at 8 mo.								
Low achievers	3.05	0.46	288	0.82	3.00	0.49	436	−0.24
Controls	3.07	0.55	1982	0.42[NS]	3.05	0.55	2677	0.39
29. Weight at 1 yr. (kg)								
Low achievers	9.89	1.14	345	0.23	9.46	1.05	486	0.11
Controls	9.87	1.21	2230	0.36[NS]	9.65	1.18	3042	0.37
30. Major malformations								
Low achievers	0.03	0.17	430	5.51	0.02	0.15	563	6.65
Controls	0.02	0.13	2579	7.65[NS]	0.01	0.10	3383	10.14
Preschool								
Age 3								
31. Abnormal language expression								
Low achievers	0.06	0.24	237	3.76	0.06	0.24	299	3.60
Controls	0.04	0.19	1212	4.96[NS]	0.03	0.16	1819	6.05
32. Abnormal speech production								
Low achievers	0.06	0.24	234	3.74	0.04	0.20	291	4.64
Controls	0.03	0.16	1211	6.12	0.02	0.12	1794	7.82
Age 4								
33. Stanford-Binet IQ								
Low achievers	95.66	11.58	361	−0.15	92.34	12.01	480	0.06
Controls	101.74	12.80	2186	0.14	95.82	11.36	3025	−0.00

(continued)

Table 1 (continued)

Variable and Group	White				Black			
	Mean	S.D.	N	Skewness	Mean	S.D.	N	Skewness
Preschool								
Age 4								
34. Graham-Ernhart Block Sort score								
Low achievers	33.80	8.07	332	−1.57	31.62	8.41	453	−1.04
Controls	35.31	7.14	2090	−1.57	33.53	7.77	2937	−1.33
35. Fine motor score								
Low achievers	78.14	16.08	324	−0.80	72.13	16.78	442	−0.13
Controls	80.83	15.60	2021	−0.93	75.23	16.28	2909	−0.34
36. Gross motor score								
Low achievers	67.36	22.13	275	−0.46	73.78	20.47	425	−0.89
Controls	71.89	21.95	1765	−0.68	75.84	19.01	2825	−0.86
37. Attention span rating								
Low achievers	2.73	0.51	357	−1.33	2.77	0.48	479	−1.54
Controls	2.82	0.48	2183	−1.53	2.85	0.42	3023	−1.71
38. Goal orientation rating								
Low achievers	2.75	0.45	357	−0.90	2.81	0.42	478	−1.33
Controls	2.83	0.44	2182	−1.03	2.88	0.41	3022	−0.85
39. Activity level rating								
Low achievers	3.12	0.61	359	0.22	3.04	0.58	478	0.19
Controls	3.02	0.57	2185	0.22	3.00	0.53	3030	0.03^{NS}
40. Dependency rating								
Low achievers	3.27	0.66	360	0.54	3.18	0.55	478	0.85
Controls	3.26	0.67	2183	0.63^{NS}	3.08	0.51	3025	0.54
41. Verbal communication rating								
Low achievers	2.93	0.64	360	0.33	2.82	0.63	478	0.11
Controls	2.90	0.64	2183	0.13^{NS}	2.92	0.63	3029	0.18
42. Suspect or abnormal behavior rating								
Low achievers	0.22	0.41	362	1.37	0.13	0.34	479	2.22
Controls	0.16	0.37	2193	1.84	0.08	0.28	3032	2.99

(continued)

Table 1 (continued)

Variable and Group	White				Black			
	Mean	S.D.	N	Skewness	Mean	S.D.	N	Skewness
Preschool								
Age 4								
43. Head circumference (cm)								
Low achievers	49.92	1.47	279	0.03 NS	49.74	1.48	419	−0.04
Controls	49.99	1.52	1927	−0.13	50.02	1.62	2691	−0.46
Seven-Year Family								
44. Socioeconomic index								
Low achievers	44.00	19.71	419	0.38	36.62	18.76	533	0.35
Controls	53.67	21.85	2553	0.02	41.47	19.15	3263	0.31
45. Housing density								
Low achievers	1.27	0.42	418	0.79	1.43	0.60	528	1.28
Controls	1.16	0.40	2547	1.20	1.36	0.62	3255	2.35
46. Number of household moves								
Low achievers	3.46	3.57	404	2.12	2.24	1.98	500	1.74
Controls	2.59	2.95	2453	3.52	1.86	1.67	3111	1.44
47. Father absent								
Low achievers	0.27	0.44	407	−1.07	0.49	0.50	500	−0.04
Controls	0.17	0.38	2462	−1.73	0.39	0.49	3116	−0.45
48. Retarded siblings								
Low achievers	0.18	0.50	404	3.49	0.14	0.43	499	3.57 NS
Controls	0.09	0.34	2432	4.14	0.10	0.37	3100	4.80
49. Maternal education (yr.)								
Low achievers	10.23	2.33	415	−0.60	10.27	2.03	525	−0.83
Controls	11.12	2.31	2499	−0.47	10.74	1.98	3224	−0.81
50. Mother employed since delivery								
Low achievers	0.64	0.48	403	−0.60	0.81	0.39	497	−1.61 NS
Controls	0.58	0.49	2429	−0.34	0.81	0.40	3100	−1.55
51. Number of younger siblings								
Low achievers	0.90	1.06	407	1.10	0.81	1.05	500	1.40 NS
Controls	1.01	1.01	2461	0.79	0.84	1.02	3113	1.31

(continued)

Table 1 (continued)

Variable and Group	White				Black			
	Mean	S.D.	N	Skewness	Mean	S.D.	N	Skewness
Seven-Year Family								
52. Number of younger half siblings								
Low achievers	0.16	0.53	405	4.46	0.29	0.70	500	2.87
Controls	0.10	0.40	2432	5.08	0.21	0.61	3097	3.43
53. Number of younger sibling deaths								
Low achievers	0.05	0.25	405	4.89	0.07	0.31	498	4.87
Controls	0.04	0.22	2431	6.08[NS]	0.04	0.22	3097	5.66
54. Family size (number of children)								
Low achievers	4.46	1.96	397	0.79	4.76	2.44	479	0.83
Controls	3.91	1.97	2385	1.63	4.14	2.17	3035	1.08
55. Day care								
Low achievers	0.61	0.49	401	−0.47	0.76	0.43	496	−1.25
Controls	0.54	0.50	2422	−0.15	0.77	0.42	3093	−1.31[NS]
56. Father employed								
Low achievers	0.87	0.34	304	−2.15	0.91	0.28	279	−2.97
Controls	0.92	0.27	2065	−3.15	0.91	0.29	2018	−2.87[NS]
57. Paternal age								
Low achievers	36.67	7.58	298	0.82	36.39	8.07	255	0.77
Controls	35.55	7.10	2037	0.93	35.56	7.55	1896	0.90[NS]
58. Public assistance								
Low achievers	0.31	0.46	403	0.85	0.37	0.48	496	0.56
Controls	0.18	0.39	2439	1.65	0.28	0.45	3097	0.97
59. Maternal mental illness								
Low achievers	0.11	0.31	339	2.57	0.06	0.24	450	3.64
Controls	0.09	0.29	2142	2.88[NS]	0.04	0.20	2843	4.67
60. Reported mental illness in study child								
Low achievers	0.02	0.14	309	7.00	0.00	0.05	423	20.57
Controls	0.00	0.05	1954	22.05	0.00	0.05	2734	21.29[NS]
Seven-Year Pediatric-Neurological								
61. Measles								
Low achievers	0.25	0.44	428	1.14	0.30	0.46	545	0.88
Controls	0.20	0.40	2572	1.49	0.29	0.45	3337	0.95[NS]

(continued)

Table 1 (continued)

Variable and Group	White				Black			
	Mean	S.D.	N	Skewness	Mean	S.D.	N	Skewness
Seven-Year Pediatric-Neurological								
62. Head trauma								
Low achievers	0.01	0.11	420	9.03	0.01	0.11	538	9.34
Controls	0.01	0.09	2523	10.58 NS	0.00	0.06	3317	16.54
63. Severe burns								
Low achievers	0.01	0.08	428	11.86	0.02	0.13	545	7.20
Controls	0.01	0.07	2572	13.97 NS	0.00	0.07	3337	14.82
64. Hemogloblin-opathy								
Low achievers	0.00	0.05	428	20.69	0.01	0.11	545	8.68
Controls	0.00	0.03	2572	35.84 NS	0.00	0.07	3337	14.82
65. Episode of "hypoxia" without unconsciousness								
Low achievers	0.01	0.11	418	9.01	0.00	0.00	544	0.00
Controls	0.00	0.06	2498	17.60	0.00	0.03	3331	33.29 NS
66. General anesthesia								
Low achievers	0.24	0.43	428	1.23	0.12	0.33	545	2.33
Controls	0.26	0.44	2572	1.13 NS	0.09	0.28	3337	2.93
67. Surgery								
Low achievers	0.32	0.47	428	0.80	0.15	0.35	545	2.02
Controls	0.30	0.46	2572	0.89 NS	0.11	0.32	3337	2.45
68. Poor coordination								
Low achievers	0.13	0.34	428	2.20	0.04	0.19	545	4.94
Controls	0.09	0.29	2572	2.78	0.05	0.21	3337	4.25 NS
69. Right-left confusion								
Low achievers	0.31	0.46	428	0.85	0.24	0.43	545	1.24
Controls	0.20	0.40	2572	1.54	0.20	0.40	3337	1.49 NS
70. Abnormal reflexes								
Low achievers	0.19	0.39	428	1.63	0.15	0.36	545	1.98
Controls	0.14	0.35	2572	2.09	0.11	0.31	3337	2.51
71. Impaired position sense								
Low achievers	0.01	0.11	428	9.12	0.02	0.12	545	8.09
Controls	0.01	0.11	2572	8.80 NS	0.01	0.07	3337	14.34

(continued)

Table 1 (continued)

Variable and Group	White				Black			
	Mean	S.D.	N	Skewness	Mean	S.D.	N	Skewness
Seven-Year Pediatric-Neurological								
72. Overall left dominance								
Low achievers	0.05	0.22	430	4.09	0.04	0.19	564	4.78
Controls	0.02	0.15	2580	6.17	0.03	0.16	3384	5.89[NS]
73. Head circumference (cm)								
Low achievers	51.25	1.52	425	0.24	51.08	1.48	544	0.30
Controls	51.33	1.57	2558	0.22[NS]	51.31	1.60	3331	0.02
Seven-Year Psychological								
74. Bender-Gestalt error score								
Low achievers	7.17	3.11	430	0.46	8.40	3.23	563	0.33
Controls	6.15	2.94	2579	0.51	7.36	3.09	3384	0.34
75. Auditory-Vocal Association score (mo.)								
Low achievers	80.86	10.82	430	0.20	73.98	10.73	563	−0.40
Controls	84.23	11.13	2570	0.45	76.83	10.00	3382	0.11
76. Draw-A-Person score								
Low achievers	90.37	11.77	430	1.08	93.29	12.08	564	0.58
Controls	94.60	11.52	2578	0.80	95.23	12.08	3384	0.63
77. Tactile Finger Recognition score, right hand								
Low achievers	4.58	0.72	429	−1.96	4.54	0.76	564	−1.97
Controls	4.67	0.62	2579	−2.06	4.63	0.65	3381	−1.86
78. Tactile Finger Recognition score, left hand								
Low achievers	4.56	0.71	429	−1.71	4.59	0.70	564	−1.96
Controls	4.72	0.56	2579	−2.13	4.64	0.66	3381	−2.04[NS]
79. Rapport with examiner rating								
Low achievers	2.97	0.63	427	−0.14	2.94	0.67	563	−0.03
Controls	2.84	0.69	2561	0.02	2.93	0.62	3380	−0.10[NS]

(continued)

Table 1 (continued)

Variable and Group	White				Black			
	Mean	S.D.	N	Skewness	Mean	S.D.	N	Skewness
Seven-Year Psychological								
80. Self-confidence rating								
Low achievers	2.65	0.57	428	−0.50	2.84	0.48	562	−0.31
Controls	2.75	0.53	2566	−0.47	2.89	0.42	3379	−1.08
81. Emotionality rating								
Low achievers	2.96	0.53	428	−0.23	2.85	0.49	563	−0.55
Controls	2.90	0.48	2567	−0.41	2.90	0.40	3378	−1.15
82. Dependency rating								
Low achievers	3.21	0.53	429	0.47	3.11	0.43	563	0.96
Controls	3.16	0.50	2567	0.89	3.05	0.39	3377	0.72
83. Attention span rating								
Low achievers	2.82	0.53	426	−0.66	2.92	0.49	564	−0.73
Controls	2.95	0.46	2563	−0.33	2.99	0.38	3373	−0.33
84. Goal orientation rating								
Low achievers	2.82	0.44	429	−1.02	2.93	0.37	563	−0.61
Controls	2.94	0.38	2561	−0.62	2.99	0.32	3374	−0.02
85. Activity level rating								
Low achievers	3.09	0.60	429	0.28	2.98	0.58	564	0.44
Controls	2.95	0.53	2568	0.19	2.97	0.46	3377	0.24[NS]
86. Verbal communication rating								
Low achievers	2.89	0.64	428	0.09	2.75	0.66	563	0.47
Controls	2.77	0.64	2565	0.23	2.76	0.58	3380	0.06[NS]
87. Assertiveness rating								
Low achievers	3.16	0.49	428	0.25	3.24	0.51	564	0.22
Controls	3.20	0.47	2564	0.57[NS]	3.19	0.44	3380	0.87
88. Suspect or abnormal behavior rating								
Low achievers	0.23	0.42	430	1.32	0.12	0.33	564	2.29
Controls	0.11	0.31	2580	2.59	0.05	0.22	3384	4.18

Note: N refers to complete data frequency

Appendix 2

VARIABLES SIGNIFICANT IN THE UNIVARIATE SCREENS AND DISCRIMINANT FUNCTION ANALYSES IN ALL COMPARISONS

Appendix 2
Variables Significant in the Univariate Screens° and Discriminant Function Analyses• in All Comparisons

	Low Achievers						Lower Achieving Subgroup						Hyperactives		IQ Subgroups		Poorest Readers
	White			Black			White			Black			Wh	Bl	Wh	Bl	
	B	G	T	B	G	T	B	G	T	B	G	T					
Prenatal Family and Maternal																	
Socioeconomic index	●	●	●	●	●	●	○	●	●	○	○	○	–	–	–	●	–
Housing density	○	○	○	○	–	○	○	●	○	○	–	○	–	–	–	–	●
Father absent[a]	–	○	○	–	–	○	–	–	–	●	–	●	–	–	●	–	–
Retarded older siblings	–	●	–	●	–	○	–	●	–	●	–	○	–	–	–	–	–
Maternal education	○	○	○	●	●	●	●	○	○	○	●	●	●	–	○	○	–
Maternal SRA score	○	–	○	–	–	–	●	–	○	–	–	–	–	–	●	●	●
Mother employed	○	○	○	–	–	–	–	○	○	–	–	–	–	–	●	○	–
Parity	●	●	●	●	○	●	○	○	●	●	–	●	–	–	–	–	–
Length of pregnancy-free interval	–	–	–	●	–	○	–	–	–	–	–	–	–	–	–	–	–
Maternal weight	–	●	○	–	–	–	–	●	○	○	–	○	○	–	–	–	–
Cigarette smoking history	–	–	○	–	–	–	–	–	–	–	–	–	–	–	–	–	–
Age at menarche	–	–	–	–	–	–	–	–	–	–	●	–	–	–	–	–	–
Maternal height	–	–	–	–	–	–	–	–	–	●	–	–	–	–	●	–	–
Retarded mother	–	–	–	–	–	–	–	●	–	–	–	–	–	–	–	–	–
Birthweight of last child	–	–	–	–	–	–	–	–	–	–	–	–	●	–	–	–	–
Last child fetal death	–	–	–	–	–	–	–	–	–	–	–	●	–	–	–	●	–
Recent maternal illnesses	–	–	–	–	–	–	–	–	–	–	–	–	–	–	○	–	–
Pregnancy and Perinatal																	
Gestation at registration	○	○	○	–	○	○	○	○	○	–	●	○	–	–	–	–	–
Hospitalizations since LMP	–	–	●	–	–	–	–	–	–	–	–	–	–	–	–	–	–
Cigarettes per day in pregnancy	●	–	○	–	–	–	–	–	–	–	●	●	–	–	–	–	–

(continued)

Appendix 2 (Continued)

	Low Achievers						Lower Achieving Subgroup						Hyper-actives		IQ Sub-groups		Poorest Readers
	White			Black			White			Black							
	B	G	T	B	G	T	B	G	T	B	G	T	Wh	Bl	Wh	Bl	
Pregnancy and Perinatal																	
Edema during pregnancy	●	–	●	–	–	–	–	–	–	–	–	–	–	–	–	–	–
Maternal heart disease during pregnancy	–	–	●	–	–	–	●	–	●	–	–	–	–	–	–	–	–
Toxemia during pregnancy	–	–	–	●	–	●	–	–	–	–	–	–	–	–	–	–	–
Urinary tract infection during pregnancy	–	–	–	●	–	–	–	–	–	–	–	–	–	–	–	–	–
Fever during pregnancy	●	–	–	–	–	–	–	–	–	–	–	–	–	–	–	–	–
Vaginal bleeding in pregnancy	–	–	–	–	–	–	–	–	–	–	–	–	–	–	●	–	–
Seizures in pregnancy	–	–	–	–	–	–	–	–	–	–	●	–	–	–	–	–	–
Anemia during pregnancy	–	●	–	–	–	–	–	○	–	–	–	–	–	–	–	–	–
Syphilis during pregnancy	–	–	–	–	●	–	–	–	–	–	–	–	–	–	–	–	–
Lowest hemoglobin in pregnancy	–	–	–	–	–	–	–	–	–	–	–	–	–	–	●	–	–
Lowest hematocrit in pregnancy	–	–	–	–	–	–	–	●	–	–	–	–	–	–	–	–	–
Hypotension during pregnancy	–	–	–	–	–	–	●	–	●	–	–	–	–	–	–	–	–
Viral infection in 1st trimester	–	●	–	–	–	–	–	–	–	–	–	–	–	–	–	–	–
Bacterial infection in 3rd trimester	–	–	–	–	–	–	–	●	–	–	–	–	–	–	–	–	–
Rubella in 3rd trimester	–	–	–	–	–	–	–	–	○	–	–	–	–	–	–	–	–

(continued)

Appendix 2 (Continued)

	Low Achievers						Lower Achieving Subgroup						Hyper-actives		IQ Sub-groups		Poorest Readers
	White			Black			White			Black			Wh	Bl	Wh	Bl	
	B	G	T	B	G	T	B	G	T	B	G	T					
Pregnancy and Perinatal																	
Inadequate pelvis	–	●	–	–	–	–	–	●	–	–	–	–	–	–	–	–	–
Number of prenatal visits	●	●	●	●	●	●	●	●	●	●	–	●	–	–	–	–	–
Weight gain during pregnancy	–	–	–	–	–	–	–	●	–	–	–	–	–	–	–	○	–
Early rupture of membranes	–	–	–	–	–	–	–	–	–	–	–	–	–	–	●	–	–
Vaginal bleeding at admission for delivery	–	–	–	–	–	–	–	–	–	–	–	–	–	–	●	–	–
Inhalation anesthetics at delivery	●	●	●	–	–	–	●	–	●	–	–	–	–	●	●	–	–
Length of 1st stage of labor	–	●	–	–	●	●	–	–	–	–	–	–	–	–	●	–	–
Length of 2nd stage of labor	–	○	–	–	–	–	–	–	–	–	–	–	–	–	○	○	–
Highest FHR in 1st stage of labor	–	–	–	–	–	–	–	–	–	–	●	–	–	–	–	–	–
Lowest FHR in 1st stage of labor	–	–	–	–	–	–	●	–	–	–	–	–	●	–	–	–	–
Highest FHR in 2nd stage of labor	–	–	–	–	–	–	–	–	–	–	–	–	–	–	–	○	–
Lowest FHR in 2nd stage of labor	–	–	–	–	●	–	–	–	–	–	●	–	–	–	–	–	–
Induction of labor	–	–	–	–	–	–	–	–	–	–	–	–	●	–	–	●	–
Arrested progress of labor	–	–	–	–	○	–	–	–	–	–	–	–	–	–	–	–	–
Augmentation of labor	–	○	–	–	–	–	–	–	–	–	–	–	–	–	○	–	–
Forceps delivery	○	○	○	–	–	–	–	–	–	–	–	–	–	–	–	–	–
Hydramnios at delivery	–	–	–	–	–	–	–	–	–	–	–	–	–	●	–	–	–
Gestational age	–	–	–	–	–	○	–	–	–	–	–	–	–	–	–	–	–

(continued)

Appendix 2 (Continued)

	Low Achievers						Lower Achieving Subgroup						Hyperactives		IQ Subgroups		Poorest Readers
	White			Black			White			Black							
	B	G	T	B	G	T	B	G	T	B	G	T	Wh	Bl	Wh	Bl	
Pregnancy and Perinatal																	
Sex of child	–	–	●	–	–	●	–	–	●	–	–	●	–	–	●	–	–
Apgar score at 1 min.	○	–	○	–	–	–	–	–	–	–	–	–	–	–	–	●	–
Apgar score at 5 min.	–	○	●	–	–	–	–	–	–	–	–	–	–	–	–	–	–
Birthweight	–	–	–	○	–	–	–	–	–	–	–	–	–	–	–	○	○
Length at birth	–	–	–	–	–	–	–	–	–	–	○	–	–	–	–	●	○
Head circumference at birth	–	–	–	●	–	–	–	–	–	–	●	–	○	–	–	○	○
Respiratory difficulty	–	–	○	–	–	–	–	–	–	–	–	–	–	–	–	–	–
Positive direct Coomb's test	–	–	–	–	–	–	–	●	–	–	–	–	–	–	–	–	–
Highest serum bilirubin	–	–	–	–	–	–	–	–	–	–	–	○	–	–	–	–	–
Resuscitation up to 5 min.	○	–	–	–	–	–	–	–	–	–	–	–	–	–	–	–	–
Lowest hematocrit of newborn	○	–	–	–	–	–	–	–	–	–	–	–	–	–	–	–	–
Lowest hemoglobin of newborn	–	–	–	–	–	–	–	●	–	–	–	–	–	–	–	–	–
Infancy																	
4 months																	
Height	–	○	–	–	–	–	–	–	–	–	–	–	–	–	–	–	–
Weight	–	●	–	○	○	–	–	–	–	–	–	–	–	–	○	○	–
Head circumference	–	–	–	●	–	–	–	–	–	–	–	–	–	–	○	–	–
8 months																	
Bayley Motor Scale score	–	–	–	–	–	●	–	–	–	–	–	–	–	–	●	–	–
Bayley Mental Scale score	–	●	–	–	–	–	–	–	–	–	–	–	–	–	–	–	–
Intensity of social response rating	–	–	–	–	–	○	–	–	–	–	–	–	–	–	●	○	–

(continued)

Appendix 2 (Continued)

	Low Achievers						Lower Achieving Subgroup						Hyper-actives		IQ Sub-groups		Poorest Readers
	White			Black			White			Black			Wh	Bl	Wh	Bl	
	B	G	T	B	G	T	B	G	T	B	G	T					
Infancy																	
8 months																	
Duration of response rating	–	–	–	–	–	–	–	–	–	–	–	–	–	–	○	●	–
Social response to mother rating	–	–	–	●	–	–	–	–	–	●	–	●	–	●	–	–	–
1 year																	
Weight	–	–	–	●	●	●	–	–	–	○	–	–	–	–	–	○	○
Height	●	–	–	○	–	–	–	–	–	○	–	–	–	–	–	–	–
Head circumference	–	–	–	●	–	–	●	–	–	○	–	–	–	–	●	–	–
Major malformations[b]	–	–	–	–	–	●	–	●	●	–	●	–	–	–	–	–	–
Congenital heart disease	–	–	–	○	–	–	–	–	–	–	–	–	–	–	–	–	–
Delayed motor development	–	–	–	–	–	–	–	–	–	–	●	–	–	–	–	–	–
Unfavorable emotional environment	–	–	–	–	●	–	–	–	–	–	–	–	–	–	–	–	○
Preschool																	
Age 3																	
Abnormal speech production	●	–	●	–	–	○	–	–	–	–	–	–	–	–	–	–	–
Abnormal language expression	–	–	–	–	●	●	–	–	–	–	●	●	–	–	–	–	–
Abnormal language reception	–	●	–	–	–	–	–	–	–	–	–	–	–	●	–	–	–
Age 4																	
Stanford-Binet IQ	●	●	●	●	●	●	●	●	●	●	●	●	–	–	●	●	●
Graham-Ernhart Block Sort score	–	○	○	–	○	●	–	–	○	–	–	○	–	–	–	○	–
Pegboard – left hand	–	–	–	–	–	–	–	●	–	–	–	–	–	–	–	–	–
Copy circle	–	–	–	–	–	–	–	–	–	–	●	–	–	–	–	–	–
Copy square	●	–	–	–	–	–	–	–	–	–	–	–	–	–	–	–	–
Fine motor score	–	–	○	○	○	○	–	–	–	–	–	–	–	–	○	●	–

(continued)

Appendix 2 (Continued)

	Low Achievers						Lower Achieving Subgroup						Hyperactives		IQ Subgroups		Poorest Readers
	White			Black			White			Black							
	B	G	T	B	G	T	B	G	T	B	G	T	Wh	Bl	Wh	Bl	
Preschool																	
Age 4																	
Hopping – right foot	–	–	–	–	–	–	–	●	–	–	–	–	–	–	–	–	–
Ball catch	●	–	–	–	–	–	–	–	–	–	–	–	–	–	–	–	–
Gross motor score	–	–	○	–	–	○	–	–	–	–	●	–	–	–	●	–	●
Attention span rating	○	–	○	–	●	○	●	–	○	–	○	–	–	○	–	–	–
Goal orientation rating	○	–	○	–	○	○	–	–	○	–	–	–	–	○	–	○	–
Activity level rating	○	–	●	–	–	–	–	–	●	–	–	–	○	●	–	○	–
Dependency rating	–	–	–	–	●	●	–	–	–	–	○	○	–	–	–	○	○
Verbal communication rating	–	–	–	–	●	○	●	–	–	–	○	●	–	–	○	–	–
Emotionality rating	–	–	–	–	–	–	–	–	–	–	–	–	●	○	–	–	○
Cooperation rating	–	–	–	–	○	–	–	–	–	●	–	–	–	–	–	○	–
Response to directions rating	–	–	–	–	○	–	–	–	–	–	○	–	–	–	–	–	●
Suspect or abnormal behavior rating	–	○	○	–	○	○	–	–	–	–	○	○	–	–	–	–	–
Head circumference	●	–	–	●	○	●	–	–	–	●	●	●	–	–	○	○	○
Height	–	–	–	–	–	–	–	–	–	–	–	–	–	–	●	○	–
Weight	○	–	–	○	–	–	–	–	–	○	–	–	–	–	●	●	–
Seven-Year Family																	
Socioeconomic index	●	●	●	○	●	●	●	●	○	○	○	○	–	–	○	●	○
Housing density	○	○	○	○	–	○	●	○	●	–	–	–	–	–	●	○	○
Number of household moves	●	○	●	●	●	●	○	–	●	●	–	●	–	–	–	–	–

(continued)

Appendix 2 (Continued)

	Low Achievers						Lower Achieving Subgroup						Hyperactives		IQ Subgroups		Poorest Readers
	White			Black			White			Black							
	B	G	T	B	G	T	B	G	T	B	G	T	Wh	Bl	Wh	Bl	
Seven-Year Family																	
Father absent[a]	○	○	○	●	○	●	–	–	○	●	–	○	–	–	–	–	–
Retarded siblings	○	●	○	○	–	–	–	–	●	○	–	–	–	–	–	–	–
Maternal education	●	○	●	●	○	○	○	○	●	○	○	●	–	–	●	○	○
Mother employed since delivery	○	–	○	–	–	–	–	–	–	–	–	–	–	○	●	–	–
Number of younger siblings	–	–	●	–	–	–	–	–	–	–	–	–	–	–	–	–	–
Number of younger half-siblings	–	●	○	○	○	○	–	–	–	●	–	○	–	–	–	–	–
Younger sibling deaths	–	–	–	○	–	○	–	○	–	○	–	○	–	○	–	–	–
Family size	●	●	●	●	○	●	○	–	○	●	○	●	–	–	○	–	–
Day care	●	–	●	–	○	–	–	–	–	–	–	–	–	–	○	–	–
Father employed	○	–	○	–	–	–	–	–	–	–	–	●	–	–	–	–	–
Paternal age	○	–	○	–	●	–	–	–	○	–	–	–	–	–	–	–	–
Public assistance	○	○	○	○	○	○	○	–	○	○	–	●	–	–	–	○	○
Mental illness in mother	–	–	–	●	–	○	●	–	○	–	–	–	–	–	–	–	–
Mental illness in study child	–	●	●	–	–	–	–	○	●	–	–	–	–	–	–	–	–
Mental illness in siblings	–	–	–	–	–	–	–	–	–	–	–	–	–	–	–	●	–
Adoptive or foster home	–	–	–	–	–	–	–	–	–	–	–	–	–	●	–	–	–
Mother's additional schooling	–	–	–	–	–	–	–	–	–	–	–	–	–	–	○	–	●
Subsequent multiple pregnancies	–	–	–	–	–	–	–	–	–	–	–	–	–	–	●	–	–
Seven-Year Pediatric-Neurological																	
Head trauma	–	–	–	●	–	●	–	–	–	–	–	–	–	–	–	–	–
Poor coordination	–	–	○	●	–	–	–	–	–	–	–	–	–	–	–	–	–
Right-left confusion	●	●	●	–	●	–	●	–	●	–	–	–	–	●	–	–	–

(continued)

Appendix 2 (Continued)

	Low Achievers						Lower Achieving Subgroup						Hyper-actives		IQ Sub-groups		Poorest Readers
	White			Black			White			Black			Wh	Bl	Wh	Bl	
	B	G	T	B	G	T	B	G	T	B	G	T					
Seven-Year Pediatric-Neurological																	
Abnormal reflexes	○	–	●	–	●	●	–	●	●	●	●	●	●	–	–	–	–
Impaired position sense	–	–	–	–	–	●	–	–	–	–	–	–	–	–	–	–	–
Overall left dominance	–	–	●	–	–	–	–	–	–	–	–	–	–	–	–	–	–
Abnormal gait	–	–	–	–	–	–	–	–	–	–	–	–	–	●	–	–	–
Impaired extra-ocular move-ments	–	–	–	–	–	–	–	–	–	–	–	–	–	●	–	–	–
Asymptomatic pure febrile seizures	–	–	–	–	–	–	–	–	–	●	–	●	–	–	–	–	–
Refractive error	–	–	–	–	–	–	–	–	–	–	–	–	–	–	–	○	–
Bilateral hearing impairment	–	–	–	–	–	–	–	–	–	–	–	●	–	–	–	–	–
"Hypoxia" with-out unconscious-ness	–	–	●	–	–	–	–	–	–	–	–	–	–	–	–	–	–
General anesthesia	–	–	–	–	–	●	–	–	–	–	–	–	–	–	–	○	–
Surgery	–	–	–	–	–	○	–	–	–	–	–	–	–	–	–	●	–
Severe burns	–	–	–	●	●	●	–	–	–	–	–	–	–	–	–	–	–
Salicylate intoxi-cation	–	●	–	–	–	–	–	–	–	–	–	–	–	–	–	–	–
Hemoglobino-pathy	–	–	–	–	–	●	–	–	–	–	–	–	–	–	–	–	–
Café au lait spots	–	–	–	–	–	–	–	–	–	–	–	–	–	–	–	●	–
Skin conditions	–	–	–	–	●	–	–	–	–	–	–	–	–	–	–	–	–
Skin infections	–	–	–	–	●	–	–	–	–	–	–	●	–	–	–	–	–
Measles	●	–	●	–	–	–	–	–	–	–	–	–	–	–	–	–	○
German measles	–	–	–	–	–	–	●	–	●	–	–	–	–	○	–	–	–
Mumps	–	–	–	–	–	–	–	–	–	–	–	–	–	–	–	●	–
Chickenpox	–	●	–	–	–	–	–	●	●	–	–	–	–	–	–	○	–
Head circum-ference	●	●	–	●	–	●	–	–	–	●	–	–	–	–	●	○	○

(continued)

Appendix 2 (Continued)

	Low Achievers						Lower Achieving Subgroup						Hyper-actives		IQ Sub-groups		Poorest Readers
	White			Black			White			Black							
	B	G	T	B	G	T	B	G	T	B	G	T	Wh	Bl	Wh	Bl	
Seven-Year Pediatric-Neurological																	
Height	–	–	–	–	–	–	–	–	–	–	–	–	–	–	–	○	–
Weight	–	–	–	–	–	–	–	–	–	–	–	–	–	–	–	●	○
Seven-Year Psychological																	
Bender-Gestalt error score	○	●	●	●	●	●	○	○	○	○	●	●	●	–	●	○	●
Auditory-Vocal Association score	●	●	●	●	●	●	–	●	●	○	–	○	–	–	●	●	●
Draw-A-Person score	●	●	●	○	●	○	●	●	●	–	–	–	–	–	●	●	○
Tactile finger recognition, right hand	–	○	○	–	–	○	–	●	●	–	–	–	–	–	–	–	–
Tactile finger recognition, left hand	●	●	●	–	–	–	○	–	●	–	–	–	–	–	–	–	–
Rapport with examiner rating	●	–	●	–	–	–	○	–	○	–	–	–	●	○	○	●	–
Self-confidence rating	●	–	●	–	○	○	●	–	●	●	○	●	–	–	●	○	–
Emotionality rating	○	–	○	–	●	●	○	–	○	●	–	●	●	●	–	–	–
Dependency rating	○	–	○	–	○	○	○	–	–	–	–	–	●	○	○	–	–
Attention span rating	○	●	○	●	–	○	○	–	○	●	–	●	●	●	○	–	●
Goal orientation rating	●	○	●	○	–	●	–	○	○	○	–	○	○	●	○	–	○
Activity level rating[c]	○	○	○	–	–	–	●	–	●	–	–	–	–	–	–	○	–
Verbal communication rating	●	–	○	–	–	–	○	–	○	–	–	–	○	○	○	○	–
Assertiveness rating	–	–	–	–	–	●	–	–	○	–	–	–	●	●	○	○	–
Separation anxiety rating	–	–	–	–	–	–	–	–	–	–	–	–	●	–	–	–	–

(continued)

Appendix 2 (Continued)

	Low Achievers						Lower Achieving Subgroup						Hyper-actives		IQ Sub-groups		Poorest Readers
	White			Black			White			Black							
	B	G	T	B	G	T	B	G	T	B	G	T	Wh	Bl	Wh	Bl	
Seven-Year Psychological																	
Fearfulness rating	–	–	–	–	–	–	●	–	●	–	–	–	○	●	○	○	–
Degree of cooperation rating	–	–	–	–	–	–	–	–	–	–	–	–	○	○	–	–	–
Frustration tolerance rating	–	–	–	○	–	–	–	–	–	○	–	○	–	–	●	–	–
Impulsivity rating	–	–	–	–	–	–	○	–	○	–	–	–	●	●	○	–	–
Hostility rating	–	–	–	–	–	–	–	–	–	–	–	–	○	○	–	–	–
Suspect or abnormal behavior rating	●	●	●	●	●	●	●	●	●	●	●	●	●	●	–	–	–
WRAT Spelling score[d]	–	–	–	–	–	–	–	–	–	–	–	–	–	●	○	○	○
WRAT Reading score[d]	–	–	–	–	–	–	–	–	–	–	–	–	–	–	○	○	–
WRAT Arithmetic score[d]	–	–	–	–	–	–	–	–	–	–	–	–	–	○	●	●	○

Note: Abbreviated group designations in column headings are Wh and Bl for white and black, B and G for boys and girls, and T for sex totals.

[a] Marital status was not included in the multivariate analyses because of its extremely high correlation with father absent, which had slightly higher associations with low achievement.

[b] This combined category includes malformations of the mouth and skin and of the musculoskeletal, cardiovascular, alimentary, and genitourinary systems.

[c] Activity level rating was not included in the analyses of hyperactive subgroups.

[d] The WRAT subtest scores were included in the analyses of hyperactive and IQ subgroups only.

Appendix 3

VARIABLES FAILING TO PASS A UNIVARIATE SCREEN IN ANY COMPARISON

Appendix 3
Variables Failing to Pass a Univariate Screen in Any Comparison

Prenatal Family and Maternal

Retarded father
Maternal mental illness
Paternal mental illness
Consanguinity
Maternal twin birth
Maternal age
Prior fetal death
Neonatal death at last delivery
Childhood death — last delivery

Pregnancy

Abdomino-pelvic x-rays
Vomiting
Jaundice
Rheumatic fever
Asthma
Diabetes
Glomerulonephritis
Rubella in 1st trimester
Rubella in 2nd trimester
Herpes hominus infection in 1st trimester
Herpes hominus infection in 2nd trimester
Herpes hominus infection in 3rd trimester
Other viral infection in 2nd trimester
Other viral infection in 3rd trimester
Toxoplasmosis
Other parasitic infection in 1st trimester
Other parasitic infection in 2nd trimester
Other parasitic infection in 3rd trimester
Fungal infection in 1st trimester
Fungal infection in 2nd trimester
Fungal infection in 3rd trimester
Bacterial infection in 1st trimester
Bacterial infection in 2nd trimester

Labor and Delivery

Vertex delivery
Breech delivery
Caesarean section
Occiput anterior presentation
Occiput posterior presentation
Abnormal presentation at delivery[a]
Placental complications
Abruptio placenta
Placenta previa
Marginal sinus rupture
Cord complications
Placental weight
Single umbilical artery
Meconium staining
Intravenous anesthetic at delivery

Neonatal

Peripheral nerve abnormality
Fractured skull
Cephalohematoma
Intracranial hemorrhage
Spinal cord abnormality
CNS infection
Brain abnormality
Erythroblastosis

(continued)

Appendix 3 (Continued)

Neonatal	
Primary apnea	Minor musculoskeletal malformations
Apneic episode	Minor eye malformations
Multiple apneic episodes	Minor ear malformations
Resuscitation after 5 minutes	Minor upper respiratory or mouth malformations
Dysmaturity	Minor alimentary malformations
Major CNS malformations	Minor skin malformations
Major eye malformations	Minor genitourinary malformations
Major thoracic malformations	Genetic or prenatal infection syndromes
Major ear malformations	Neonatal seizures
Minor CNS malformations	Multiple birth
Eight Months	
Speed of response rating	Social response to examiner rating
Intensity of response rating	Activity level rating
Persistence in pursuit rating	
One Year	
Subdural hematoma	Loss of one or both parents
Other intracranial hemorrhage	Foster home
CNS infection or inflammation	Prolonged or recurrent hospitalization
Hypoxia	Failure to thrive
Head trauma	Cerebral palsy
Cord disease	Dyskinesia or ataxia
Lead intoxication	Febrile seizures
Hypotonia	Nonfebrile seizures
Peripheral nerve abnormality	Spasmus nutans
Visual impairment	Hypothyroidism
Strabismus	Other endocrine or metabolic disease
Nystagmus	
Age Three	
Abnormal hearing	

(continued)

Appendix 3 (Continued)

Age Four	
Line walk	Impulsivity rating
Hopping — left foot	Right handedness
Wallin pegboard — right hand	Left handedness
Copy cross	Indeterminate handedness
Stringing beads	Right dominance
Porteus maze IV	Left dominance
Irritability rating	Mixed dominance
Seven-Year Family	
Number of children under 8 in household	Number of subsequent fetal deaths
Number of subsequent pregnancies	Paternal mental illness
Seven-Year Pediatric-Neurological	
Cord disease	Eczema
Amblyopia	Gonadal dysgenesis
Color blindness	Battered child
Visual field defect	Spasmus nutans
Nystagmus	Failure to thrive
Cranial nerve abnormality	Hypothyroidism
Other sensory abnormality	Septicemia
Coma	Bacterial meningitis
Abnormal shape of skull	Nonbacterial meningitis
Subdural hematoma or effusion	Encephalitis
Other intracranial hemorrhage	Other CNS infection
Chorioretinitis	Respiratory infection
Retrolental fibroplasia	Genitourinary tract infection
Asthma	Bone or joint infection
Acyanotic congenital heart disease	Heart infection
Cyanotic congenital heart disease	Severe diarrhea
Rheumatic heart disease	Liver infection
Documented cardiovascular disorder	Eye infection
Hemolytic disease	Ear infection
Coagulation defect	Roseola
Major hemorrhage	Whooping cough
Anemia	Other childhood diseases
Other hematologic disorder	Recurrent or chronic infection

(continued)

Appendix 3 (Continued)

Seven-Year Pediatric-Neurological	
Fractured skull, linear	Dystonia
Fractured skull, other	Ballismus
Other fractures	Tic
Symptomatic hydrocarbon intoxication	Mirror movements
Lead intoxication	Other abnormal movements
Other symptomatic intoxication	Right handedness
Reaction to immunization	Left handedness
Other trauma or intoxication	Indeterminate handedness
Shock requiring hospitalization	Right dominance
Severe dehydration	Mixed dominance
Electrolyte imbalance	Cerebral palsy
Hyperthermia	Dyskinesia or ataxia
Hypoxia with unconsciousness	Petit mal
Diagnostic or other medical procedures	Atypical staring
Cystic fibrosis	Minor motor seizures
Diabetes	Asymptomatic generalized seizures
Other endocrine or metabolic disorders	Asymptomatic partial seizures
Astereognosis	Syncope
Fasciculations	Epilepsy
Myoclonus	Isolated nonfebrile seizures
Spontaneous tremor	Asymptomatic complex febrile seizures
Intention tremor	Monocular blindness
Athetosis	Binocular blindness
Chorea	

[a]Face, chin, brow, or shoulder

Appendix 4

DISCRIMINANT FUNCTION ANALYSES WITH STUDY CENTERS INCLUDED

Table 1
Distribution of Low Achievers and Controls by Study Center

	White			Black		
	Low Achievers	Controls	χ^2	Low Achievers	Controls	χ^2
Boston Lying-In Hospital	30.2%	45.1%	32.54****	2.8%	6.2%	9.68**
Providence Lying-In Hospital	17.2	9.8	20.37****	4.6	2.7	5.33*
Children's Hospital, Buffalo	3.3	9.5	17.47***	0.0	0.3	0.71
Columbia-Presbyterian Medical Center	1.4	2.7	2.09	3.4	4.5	1.21
New York Medical College	0.2	0.3	0.04	2.5	2.4	0.00
Pennsylvania Hospital	4.0	3.2	0.41	34.6	33.0	0.47
Johns Hopkins Hospital	8.6	3.2	27.17****	17.2	13.2	6.35*
Medical College of Virginia	3.7	3.6	0.00	6.0	10.6	10.69**
University of Tennessee College of Medicine	0.0	0.0	—	13.3	14.9	0.86
Charity Hospital, New Orleans	0.0	0.0	—	9.6	8.1	1.20
University of Minnesota Hospital	9.1	13.0	5.01*	0.2	0.1	0.01
University of Oregon Medical School	22.3	9.6	57.60****	5.8	4.0	3.67
Total	100.0%	100.0%		100.0%	100.0%	
N	430	2580		564	3384	
Overall χ^2	141.76****			41.70****		

*$p < .05$; **$p < .01$; ***$p < .0001$; ****$p < .00001$

Table 2
All Discriminators Between Low Achievers and Controls with Study Centers Entered

	Standardized Coefficient	
	White	Black
Percent male	.29	.53
Rapport with examiner rating (7 yr.)	.25	—
Johns Hopkins	.25	—
Mental illness in study child	.21	—
Socioeconomic index (prenatal)	−.20	—
Oregon	.20	—
Parity	.19	—
Suspect or abnormal behavior rating (7 yr.)	.19	.25
Providence	.19	—
Draw-A-Person score	−.18	—
Self-confidence rating (7 yr.)	−.18	—
Tactile Finger Recognition, left	−.17	—
Stanford-Binet IQ	−.16	—
Right-left confusion	.15	—
Goal orientation rating (7 yr.)	−.15	—
Apgar score (5 min.)	−.13	—
Left dominance	.13	—
Maternal heart disease during pregnancy	.11	—
Inhalation anesthetics at delivery	.11	—
Day care	.10	—
Prenatal visits	−.08	−.16
Bender-Gestalt error score	—	.25
Family size	—	.24
Length of 1st stage of labor	—	.21
Weight at 1 yr.	—	−.19
Household moves	—	.18
Abnormal language expression (3 yr.)	—	.16
Maternal education (prenatal)	—	−.15
Assertiveness rating (7 yr.)	—	.14
Dependency rating (4 yr.)	—	.14
Auditory-Vocal Association score	—	−.14
Virginia	—	−.14
Toxemia during pregnancy	—	.13
Severe burns	—	.13
Father absent (7 yr.)	—	.13

(continued)

Table 2 (Continued)

	Standardized Coefficient	
	White	Black
Head circumference (4 yr.)	—	−.13
Impaired position sense	—	.12
Hemoglobinopathy	—	.12
Abnormal reflexes	—	.11
Major malformations	—	.09
Canonical correlation	.38	.32
χ^2	460.13*	412.64*
Correct group classification (N)		
Low achievers	(430) 68.6%	(564) 63.8%
Controls	(2580) 73.9%	(3384) 70.7%

*$p < .00001$

Table 3
Sex Differences in All Discriminators in the White Sample with Study Centers Entered

	Standardized Coefficient	
	Boys	Girls
Socioeconomic index (prenatal)	−.33	—
Self-confidence rating (7 yr.)	−.30	—
Abnormal speech production (3 yr.)	.26	—
Rapport with examiner rating (7 yr.)	.25	—
Day care	.23	—
Family size	.22	—
Johns Hopkins	.22	.26
Goal orientation rating (7 yr.)	−.21	—
Failure on ball catch	.20	—
Right-left confusion	.20	—
Draw-A-Person score	−.19	−.23
Verbal communication rating (7 yr.)	.19	—
Inhalation anesthetics at delivery	.18	—
Head circumference (7 yr.)	−.14	—
Suspect or abnormal behavior rating (7 yr.)	.14	.23
Tactile Finger Recognition, left	−.14	−.20
Mental illness in study child	—	.31
Oregon	—	.28
Inadequate pelvis	—	.26
Stanford-Binet IQ	—	−.26
Providence	—	.26
Salicylate intoxication	—	.20
Pre-pregnant weight	—	.19
Viral infection in 1st trimester	—	.19
Prenatal visits	—	−.17
Parity	—	.14
Retardation in older siblings	—	.14
Canonical correlation	.36	.40
χ^2	217.79*	250.89*
Correct group classification (N)		
Low achievers	(297) 66.0%	(133) 66.9%
Controls	(1276) 71.1%	(1304) 79.5%

*$p < .00001$

Table 4
All Discriminators for Boys in the Black Sample with Study Centers Entered

	Standardized Coefficient
Head circumference (7 yr.)	−.40
Household moves	.32
Family size	.32
Suspect or abnormal behavior rating (7 yr.)	.25
Retardation in older siblings	.22
Auditory-Vocal Association score	−.21
Attention span rating (7 yr.)	−.21
Bender-Gestalt error score	.20
Poor coordination	−.20
Social response to mother rating (8 mo.)	.19
Virginia	−.19
Head trauma	.17
Urinary tract infection during pregnancy	.15
Pregnancy-free interval	−.14
Maternal mental illness	.12
Prenatal visits	−.12
Canonical correlation	.31
χ^2	196.03*
Correct group classification (N)	
Low achievers (379)	59.9%
Controls (1554)	69.6%

$^*p < .00001$

Table 5
Distribution of the Lower Achieving Subgroup and Controls by Study Center

	White			Black		
	Lower Achieving Subgroup	Controls	χ^2	Lower Achieving Subgroup	Controls	χ^2
Boston Lying-In Hospital	39.7%	45.7%	1.90	4.6%	6.1%	0.38
Providence Lying-In Hospital	14.7	8.6	6.15*	4.1	2.5	1.06
Children's Hospital, Buffalo	1.9	9.6	9.57**	0.0	0.4	0.03
Columbia-Presbyterian Medical Center	1.3	2.7	0.67	2.3	4.6	1.46
New York Medical College	0.0	0.3	0.01	3.5	2.3	0.56
Pennsylvania Hospital	5.8	3.1	2.56	31.4	33.4	0.21
Johns Hopkins Hospital	7.1	3.0	6.76**	18.0	13.2	2.84
Medical College of Virginia	4.5	3.8	0.05	7.0	10.3	1.63
University of Tennessee College of Medicine	0.0	0.0	—	10.5	14.5	1.85
Charity Hospital, New Orleans	0.0	0.0	—	12.2	8.3	2.72
University of Minnesota Hospital	6.4	13.1	5.30*	0.0	0.1	0.78
University of Oregon Medical School	18.6	10.1	10.50**	6.4	4.3	1.24
Total	100.0%	100.0%		100.0%	100.0%	
N	156	2964		172	3096	
Overall χ^2	45.07***			16.92		

$^*p < .05$; $^{**}p < .01$; $^{***}p < .00001$

Table 6
All Discriminators Between the Lower Achieving Subgroup and Controls in the White Sample with Study Centers Entered

	Standardized Coefficient
Suspect or abnormal behavior rating (7 yr.)	.30
Mental illness in study child	.30
Percent male	.28
Fearfulness rating (7 yr.)	−.25
Draw-A-Person score	−.23
Prenatal visits	−.21
Maternal heart disease during pregnancy	.21
Socioeconomic index (prenatal)	−.20
Self-confidence rating (7 yr.)	−.19
Housing density	.18
Inhalation anesthetics at delivery	.16
Activity rating (7 yr.)	.15
German measles	−.15
Tactile Finger Recognition, left	−.14
Right-left confusion	.14
Minnesota	−.14
Major malformations	.13
Retardation in siblings	.13
Johns Hopkins	.11
Canonical correlation	.27
χ^2	236.16*
Correct group classification (N)	
Low achievers (156)	64.1%
Controls (2964)	77.8%

*$p < .00001$

Table 7
All Discriminators for Girls in the White Subgroup with Study Centers Entered

	Standardized Coefficient
Inadequate pelvis	.36
Bacterial infection in 3rd trimester	.32
Suspect or abnormal behavior rating (7 yr.)	.30
Stanford-Binet IQ	−.30
Positive Coombs, newborn	.25
Providence	.24
Prepregnant weight	.21
Retardation in mother	.21
Draw-A-Person score	−.20
Failure on pegboard, left	.19
Failure to hop, right	.19
Weight gain during pregnancy	.18
Major malformations	.18
Abnormal reflexes	.18
Johns Hopkins	.18
Canonical correlation	.31
χ^2	152.84*
Correct group classification (N)	
Low achievers (45)	66.7%
Controls (1495)	85.4%

*$p < .00001$

Table 8
All Discriminators Between Hyperactives and Non-Hyperactives with Study Centers Entered

	Standardized Coefficient	
	White	Black
Suspect or abnormal behavior rating (7 yr.)	.38	.40
Impulsivity rating (7 yr.)	.33	.28
Rapport with examiner rating (7 yr.)	.29	—
Johns Hopkins	.28	—
Attention span rating (7 yr.)	−.26	−.17
Assertiveness rating (7 yr.)	−.23	−.14
Induction of labor	−.20	—
Dependency rating (7 yr.)	.19	—
Emotionality rating (4 yr.)	.14	—
Bender-Gestalt error score	.14	—
Hydramnios at delivery	—	.34
Fearfulness rating (7 yr.)	—	−.20
Abnormal gait	—	.20
Goal orientation rating (7 yr.)	—	−.18
Emotionality rating (7 yr.)	—	.18
Inhalation anesthetics at delivery	—	.13
Oregon	—	.12
Canonical correlation	.59	.65
χ^2	177.27*	300.90*
Correct group classification(N)		
Hyperactives	(80) 75.0%	(70) 72.9%
Non-Hyperactives	(349) 86.5%	(494) 94.3%

*$p < .00001$

Table 9
All Discriminators Among IQ Groups with Study Centers Entered

	Standardized Coefficient	
	White	Black
Auditory-Vocal Association score	.42	.29
WRAT arithmetic score	.34	.30
Intensity of social response rating (8 mo.)	.25	—
Bender-Gestalt error score	.25	—
Vaginal bleeding in pregnancy	.24	—
Head circumference (7 yr.)	.24	—
Draw-A-Person score	.21	—
Boston	.21	.38
Self-confidence rating (7 yr.)	.18	—
Maternal SRA score	.14	—
Frustration tolerance rating (7 yr.)	.13	—
Subsequent multiple pregnancies	.10	—
Gross motor score	.03	—
Stanford-Binet IQ	—	.27
Rapport with examiner rating (7 yr.)	—	.26
Fine motor score	—	.21
Mental illness in siblings	—	.21
Induction of labor	—	.17
Prior fetal death	—	.14
Café au lait spots	—	.13
Duration of response rating (8 mo.)	—	.10
Surgery	—	.10
Apgar score (1 min.)	—	.09
Mumps	—	.08
Columbia	—	.06
Pennsylvania	—	.03
Canonical correlation	.52	.53
χ^2	186.54*	249.61*
Correct group classification (N)		
Low IQ	(184) 61.4%	(286) 64.3%
Medium IQ	(182) 51.6%	(236) 53.8%
High IQ	(64) 57.8%	(42) 69.0%

$*p < .00001$

References

Adams, R. M., Kocsis, J. J., & Estes, R. E. (1974). Soft neurological signs in learning-disabled children and controls. *American Journal of Diseases of Children, 128,* 614–618.

Alberman, E. (1973). The early prediction of learning disorders. *Developmental Medicine and Child Neurology, 15,* 202–204.

Ayres, A. J. (1972). Types of sensory integrative dysfunction among disabled learners. *American Journal of Occupational Therapy, 26,* 13–18.

Bakker, D. J. (1972). *Temporal order in disturbed reading.* Rotterdam: University Press.

Bakwin, H. (1973). Reading disability in twins. *Developmental Medicine and Child Neurology, 15,* 184–187.

Barkley, R. (1981). Specific guidelines for defining hyperactivity in children. In B. Lahey & A. Kaydin (Eds.), *Advancement in clinical child psychology* (Vol. IV). New York: Plenum.

Barlow, C. F. (1974). "Soft signs" in children with learning disorders. *American Journal of Diseases of Children, 128,* 605–606.

Bauer, R. H. (1977a). Memory processes in children with learning disabilities: Evidence for deficient rehearsal. *Journal of Experimental Child Psychology, 24,* 415–430.

Bauer, R. H. (1977b). Short-term memory in learning disabled and nondisabled children. *Bulletin of the Psychonomic Society, 10,* 128–130.

Bell, A. E., Abrahamson, D. S., & McRae, K. N. (1977). Reading retardation: A 12-year prospective study. *Journal of Pediatrics, 91,* 363–370.

Bell, A. E., Aftanas, M. S., & Abrahamson, D. S. (1976). Scholastic progress of children from different socio-economic groups, matched for IQ. *Developmental Medicine and Child Neurology, 18,* 717–727.

Belmont, L. (1980). Epidemiology. In H. E. Rie & E. D. Rie (Eds.), *Handbook of minimal brain dysfunctions: A critical view.* New York: Wiley.

Belmont, I., & Belmont, L. (1978). Stability or change in reading achievement over time: Developmental and eduational implications. *Journal of Learning Disabilities, 11,* 31–39.

Belmont, L., & Birch, H. G. (1965). Lateral dominance, lateral awareness, and reading disability. *Child Development, 36,* 57–71.

Belmont, L., & Birch, H. G. (1966). The intellectual profile of retarded readers. *Perceptual and Motor Skills, 22,* 787–816.

Belmont, L., Stein, Z. A., & Wittes, J. T. (1976). Birth order, family size and school failure. *Developmental Medicine and Child Neurology, 18,* 421–430.

Bender, L. (1956). *Psychopathology of children with organic brain disorders.* Springfield, IL: Charles C. Thomas.

Bender, L. (1957). Specific reading disability as a maturational lag. *Bulletin of the Orton Society, 7,* 9–18.

Bender, L. (1975). A career of clinical research in child psychiatry. In E. J. Anthony (Ed.), *Explorations in child psychiatry.* New York: Plenum.

Benton, A. L. (1958). Significance of systematic reversal in right–left discrimination. *Acta Psychiatrica et Neurologica Scandinavica, 33,* 129–137.

Benton, A. L. (1975). Developmental dyslexia: Neurological aspects. In W. J. Friedlander (Ed.), *Advances in neurology* (Vol. 7). New York: Raven Press.

Benton, A. L. (1978). Some conclusions about dyslexia. In A. L. Benton & D. Pearl (Eds.), *Dyslexia: An appraisal of current knowledge.* New York: Oxford University Press.

Benton, A. L., & Pearl, D. (Eds.). (1978). *Dyslexia: An appraisal of current knowledge.* New York: Oxford University Press.

Berler, E. S., & Romanczyk, R. G. (1980). Assessment of the learning disabled and hyperactive child: An analysis and critique. *Journal of Learning Disabilities, 13,* 536–538.

Birch, H. G. (1962). Dyslexia and maturation of visual function. In J. Money (Ed.), *Reading disability: Progress and research needs in dyslexia.* Baltimore: Johns Hopkins Press.

Bishop, D. V. M. (1979). Comprehension in developmental language disorders. *Developmental Medicine and Child Neurology, 21,* 225–238.

Boder, E. (1976). School failure—evaluation and treatment. *Pediatrics, 58,* 394–403.

Bradley, J. V. (1968). *Distribution-free statistical tests.* Englewood Cliffs, NJ: Prentice–Hall.

Bradley, L., & Bryant, P. E. (1979). Independence of reading and spelling in backward and normal readers. *Developmental Medicine and Child Neurology, 21,* 504–514.

Brenner, M. W., Gillman, S., Zangwill, O. L., & Farrell, M. (1967). Visuo-motor disability in schoolchildren. *British Medical Journal, 4,* 259–262.

Broman, S. H. (1981). Long-term development of children born to teenagers. In K. G. Scott, T. Field, & E. G. Robertson (Eds.), *Teenage parents and their offspring.* New York: Grune & Stratton.

Broman, S. H. (1984). The Collaborative Perinatal Project: An overview. In S. A. Mednick, M. Harway, & K. M. Finello (Eds.), *Handbook of longitudinal research (Vol. I).* New York: Praeger.

Broman, S. H., Nichols, P. L., & Kennedy, W. A. (1975). *Preschool IQ: Prenatal and early developmental correlates.* Hillsdale, NJ: Lawrence Erlbaum Associates.

Bryan, T., & Bryan, J. H. (1980). Learning disorders. In H. E. Rie & E. D. Rie (Eds.), *Handbook of minimal brain dysfunctions: A critical view.* New York: Wiley.

Cantwell, D. P. (1980). Drugs and medical intervention. In H. E. Rie & E. D. Rie (Eds.), *Handbook of minimal brain dysfunctions: A critical view.* New York; Wiley.

Caplan, H., Bibace, R., & Rabinovitch, M. S. (1963). Paranatal stress, cognitive organization and ego function: A controlled follow-up study of children born prematurely. *Journal of the American Academy of Child Psychiatry, 2,* 434–450.

Cermak, L. S., Goldberg–Warter, J., DeLuca, D., Cermak, S., & Drake, C. (1981). The role of interference in the verbal retention ability of learning-disabled children. *Journal of Learning Disabilities, 14,* 291–295.

Clements, S. D. (1966). *Minimal brain dysfunction in children* (NINDB Monograph No. 3, U.S. Public Health Service Publication No. 1415). Washington, DC: U.S. Government Printing Office.

Clements, S. D., & Peters, J. E. (1962). Minimal brain dysfunctions in the school-age child. *Archives of General Psychiatry, 6,* 185–197.

Conners, C. K. (1978). Critical review of "Electroencephalographic and neurophysiological studies in dyslexia." In A. L. Benton & D. Pearl (Eds.), *Dyslexia: An appraisal of current knowledge*. New York: Oxford University Press.

Corah, N. L., Anthony, E. J., Painter, P., Stern, J. A., & Thurston, D. L. (1965). Effects of perinatal anoxia after seven years. *Psychological Monographs, 79,* (3, whole No. 596).

Crinella, F. M., Beck, F. W., & Robinson, J. W. (1971). Unilateral dominance is not related to neuropsychological integrity. *Child Development, 42,*2033–2054.

Critchley, M. (1964). *Developmental dyslexia*. London: William Heinemann.

Critchley, M. (1970). *The dyslexic child*. Springfield, IL: Charles C Thomas.

Cruickshank, W. M. (1968). The problems of delayed recognition and its correction. In A. H. Keeney & V. T. Keeney (Eds.), *Dyslexia: Diagnosis and the treatment of reading disorders*. St. Louis: Mosby.

Cruickshank, W. M. (1977). Myths and realities in learning disabilities. *Journal of Learning Disabilities, 10,* 51–58.

Cruickshank, W. M. (1983). Learning disabilities: A neurophysiological dysfunction. *Journal of Learning Disabilities, 16,* 27–29.

Cruickshank, W. M., Bentzen, F. A., Ratzberg, F. H., & Tannhauser, M. T. (1961). *A teaching method for brain-injured and hyperactive children*. Syracuse, NY: Syracuse University Press.

Davie, R., Butler, N., & Goldstein, H. (1972). *From birth to seven: A report of the National Child Development Study*. London: Longman.

Dearman, N. B., & Plisko, V. W. (1980). *The condition of education: 1980 Edition* (Statistical Report, National Center for Education Statistics). Washington, DC: U.S. Government Printing Office.

DeFries, J. C., Singer, S. M., Foch, T. T., & Lewitter, F. I. (1978). Familial nature of reading disability. *British Journal of Psychiatry, 132,* 361–367.

Delamater, A. M., Lahey, B. B., & Drake, L. (1981). Toward an empirical subclassification of "learning disabilities": A psychophysiological comparison of "hyperactive" and "non-hyperactive" subgroups. *Journal of Abnormal Child Psychology, 9,* 65–77.

Denckla, M. B. (1978). Critical review of "Electroencephalographic and neurophysiological studies in dyslexia." In A. L. Benton & D. Pearl (Eds.), *Dyslexia: An appraisal of current knowledge*. New York: Oxford University Press.

de Quiros, J. B. (1976). Diagnosis of vestibular disorders in the learning disabled. *Journal of Learning Disabilities, 9,* 39–47.

Douglas, J. W. B. (1975). Early hospital admissions and later disturbances of behaviour and learning. *Developmental Medicine and Child Neurology, 17,* 456–480.

Eisenberg, L. (1975). Psychiatric aspects of language disability. In D. D. Duane & M. B. Rawson (Eds.), *Reading, perception and language*. Baltimore: York Press.

Eisenberg, L. (1978). Definitions of dyslexia: Their consequences for research and policy. In A. L. Benton & D. Pearl (Eds.), *Dyslexia: An appraisal of current knowledge*. New York: Oxford University Press.

Elkins, J., & Sultmann, W. F. (1981). ITPA and learning disability: A discriminant analysis. *Journal of Learning Disabilities, 14,* 88–92.

Eme, R. F. (1979). Sex differences in childhood psychopathology: A review. *Psychological Bulletin, 86,* 574–595.

Feagans, L. (1983). A current view of learning disabilities. *Journal of Pediatrics, 102,* 487–493.

Finlayson, M. A. J., & Reitan, R. M. (1976). Tactile-perceptual functioning in relation to intellectual, cognitive, and reading skills in younger and older normal children. *Developmental Medicine and Child Neurology, 18,* 442–446.

Finucci, J. M., Guthrie, J. T., Childs, A. L., Abbey, H., & Childs, B. (1976). The genetics of specific reading disability. *Annals of Human Genetics, 40,* 1–23.

Fletcher, J. M. (1983). External validation of learning disability typologies. In B. P. Rourke (Ed.), *Subtype analysis of learning disabilities.* New York: Guilford.

Francis–Williams, J. (1976). Early identification of children likely to have specific learning difficulties: Report of a follow-up. *Developmental Medicine and Child Neurology, 18,* 71–77.

Freides, D., Barbati, J., van Kempen–Horowitz, L. J., Sprehn, G., Iversen, C., Silver, J. R., & Woodward, R. (1980). Blind evaluation of body reflexes and motor skills in learning disability. *Journal of Autism and Developmental Disorders, 10,* 159–171.

Friedman, E. A., & Neff, R. K. (1977). *Pregnancy hypertension: A systematic evaluation of clinical diagnostic criteria.* Littleton, MA: Publishing Sciences Group.

Frostig, M. (1972). Visual perception, integrative functions, and academic learning. *Journal of Learning Disabilities, 5,* 1–15.

Galante, M. B., Flye, M. E., & Stephens, L. S. (1972). Cumulative minor deficits: A longitudinal study of the relation of physical factors to school achievement. *Journal of Learning Disabilities, 5,* 75–80.

Goldstein, M., & Dillon, W. R. (1978). *Discrete discriminant analysis.* New York: Wiley.

Goodman, P. (1964). *Compulsory mis-education.* New York: Vintage Books.

Grizzle, J. E. (1967). Continuity correction in the χ^2-test for 2×2 tables. *The American Statistician, 21,* 28–32.

Gross, M. B., & Wilson, W. C. (1974). *Minimal brain dysfunction.* New York: Brunner/Mazel.

Haller, J. S., & Axelrod, P. (1975). Minimal brain dysfunction syndrome. *American Journal of Diseases of Children, 129,* 1319–1324.

Hallgren, B. (1950). Specific dyslexia ("congenital word blindness"). A clinical and genetic study. *Acta Psychiatrica et Neurologica,* Supplement 65, 1–287.

Hardy, J. B., Drage, J. S., & Jackson, E. C. (1979). *The first year of life.* Baltimore: Johns Hopkins Press.

Hermann, K. (1959). *Reading disability: A medical study of word-blindness and related handicaps.* Springfield, IL: Charles C Thomas.

Hoffman, L. W. (1979). Maternal employment: 1979. *American Psychologist, 34,* 859–865.

Hughes, J. R. (1978). Electroencephalographic and neurophysiological studies in dyslexia. In A. L. Benton & D. Pearl (Eds.), *Dyslexia: An appraisal of current knowledge.* New York: Oxford University Press.

Illingworth, R. S. (1980). Developmental variations in relation to minimal brain dysfunction. In H. E. Rie & E. D. Rie (Eds.), *Handbook of minimal brain dysfunctions: A critical view.* New York: Wiley.

Isom, J. B. (1968). Some neuropsychological findings in children with reading problems. In M. P. Douglass (Ed.), *Claremont Reading Conference,* (32nd Yearbook). Claremont, CA: Claremont University Center.

Jastak, J. F., & Jastak, S. R. (1965). *The Wide Range Achievement Test: Manual of instructions.* Wilmington: Guidance Associates.

Johnson, D. J., & Myklebust, H. R. (1967). *Learning disabilities.* New York: Grune & Stratton.

Jordan, T. E. (1964). Early developmental adversity and classroom learning: A prospective inquiry. *American Journal of Mental Deficiency, 69,* 360–371.

Kappelman, M. M., Rosenstein, A. B., & Ganter, R. L. (1972). Comparison of disadvantaged children with learning disabilities and their successful peer group. *American Journal of Diseases of Children, 124,* 875–879.

Kawi, A. A., & Pasamanick, B. (1958). Association of factors of pregnancy with reading disorders in childhood. *Journal of the American Medical Association, 166,* 1420–1423.

Kawi, A. A., & Pasamanick, B. (1959). Prenatal and paranatal factors in the development of childhood reading disorders. *Monographs of the Society for Research in Child Development, 24* (4, Serial No. 73), 184–188.

Kenny, T. J. (1980). Hyperactivity. In H. E. Rie & E. D. Rie (Eds.), *Handbook of minimal brain dysfunctions: A critical view.* New York: Wiley.

Kephart, N. C. (1960). *The slow learner in the classroom*. Columbus, OH: Merrill.

Kessler, J. W. (1980). History of minimal brain dysfunctions. In H. E. Rie & E. D. Rie (Eds.), *Handbook of minimal brain dysfunctions: A critical view*. New York: Wiley.

Kinsbourne, M. (1973). School problems. *Pediatrics, 52*, 697–710.

Kirk, S. A. (1962). *Educating exceptional children*. Boston: Houghton Mifflin.

Kirk, S. A., & Bateman, B. (1962). Diagnosis and remediation of learning disabilities. *Exceptional Children, 29*, 73–78.

Kirk, S. A., & Elkins, J. (1975). Characteristics of children enrolled in the Child Service Demonstration Centers. *Journal of Learning Disabilities, 8*, 630–637.

Klasen, E. (1972). *The syndrome of specific dyslexia*. Baltimore: University Park Press.

Klecka, W. R. (1979). Discriminant analysis. *Sage University Paper Series on Quantitative Applications in the Social Sciences*. Beverly Hills and London: Sage.

Klein, P. S., Forbes, G. B., & Nader, P. R. (1975). Effects of starvation in infancy (pyloric stenosis) on subsequent learning abilities. *The Journal of Pediatrics, 87*, 8–15.

Knoke, J. D. (1982). Discriminant analysis with discrete and continuous variables. *Biometrics, 38*, 191–200.

Kohn, M. (1977). *Social competence, symptoms, and underachievement in childhood: A longitudinal perspective*. Washington, DC: Winston.

Lahey, B. B., Stempniak, M., Robinson, E. J., & Tyroler, M. J. (1978). Hyperactivity and learning disabilities as independent dimensions of child behavior problems. *Journal of Abnormal Psychology, 87*, 333–340.

Lassman, F. M., Fisch, R. O., Vetter, D. C., & LaBenz, E. S. (1980). *Early correlates of speech, language and hearing*. Littleton, MA: Publishing Sciences Group.

Leviton, A. (1980). Otitis media and learning disorders. *Journal of Developmental and Behavioral Pediatrics, 1*, 58–63.

Lilienfeld, A. M., & Pasamanick, B. (1955). The association of maternal and fetal factors with the development of cerebral palsy and epilepsy. *American Journal of Obstetrics and Gynecology, 70*, 93–101.

Lucas, A. R. (1980). Muscular control and coordination in minimal brain dysfunctions. In H. E. Rie & E. D. Rie (Eds.), *Handbook of minimal brain dysfunctions: A critical view*. New York: Wiley.

Ludlow, C. L. (1980). Children's language disorders: Recent research advances. *Annals of Neurology, 7*, 497–507.

Lyle, J. G. (1970). Certain antenatal, perinatal, and developmental variables and reading retardation in middle-class boys. *Child Development, 41*, 481–491.

Maccoby, E. E., & Jacklin, C. N. (1974). *The psychology of sex differences*. Stanford, CA: Stanford University Press.

Makita, K. (1968). The rarity of reading disability in Japanese children. *American Journal of Orthopsychiatry, 38*, 599–614.

Masters, L., & Marsh, G. E. (1978). Middle ear pathology as a factor in learning disabilities. *Journal of Learning Disabilities, 11*, 103–106.

McMahon, R. C. (1981). Biological factors in childhood hyperkinesis. *Journal of Clinical Psychology, 37*, 12–21.

Mendenhall, W., & Ott, L. (1980). *Understanding statistics*. Belmont, CA: Wadsworth.

Menkes, J. H. (1974). The clinical evaluation of school difficulties. *Neuropadiatrie, 5*, 217–223.

Mercer, C. D., Forgnone, C., & Wolking, W. D. (1976). Definitions of learning disabilities used in the United States. *Journal of Learning Disabilities, 9*, 376–386.

Mosteller, F., & Tukey, J. W. (1977). *Data analysis and regression*. Reading, MA: Addison–Wesley.

Myklebust, H. R. (1968). Learning disabilities: Definition and overview. In H. R. Myklebust (Ed.), *Progress in learning disabilities* (Vol. I). New York: Grune & Stratton.

Myrianthopoulos, N. C., & French, K. S. (1968). An application of the U.S. Bureau of the Census socioeconomic index to a large, diversified patient population. *Social Science and Medicine, 2,* 283–299.

Naylor, H. (1980). Reading disability and lateral asymmetry: An information-processing analysis. *Psychological Bulletin, 87,* 531–545.

Nichols, P. L., & Chen, T. C. (1981). *Minimal brain dysfunction: A prospective study.* Hillsdale, NJ: Lawrence Erlbaum Associates.

Niswander, K. R., & Gordon, M. (Eds.). (1972). *The women and their pregnancies.* Philadelphia: Saunders.

Norman, C. A., & Zigmond, N. (1980). Characteristics of children labeled and served as learning disabled in school systems affiliated with Child Service Demonstration Centers. *Journal of Learning Disabilities, 13,* 542–547.

Omenn, G. S. (1973). Genetic issues in the syndrome of minimal brain dysfunction. In S. Walzer & P. H. Wolff (Eds.), *Minimal cerebral dysfunction in children.* New York: Grune & Stratton.

Orton, S. T. (1925). "Word-blindness" in school children. *Archives of Neurology and Psychiatry, 14,* 581–615.

Orton, S. T. (1937). *Reading, writing and speech problems in children.* New York: Norton.

Owen, F. W. (1978). Dyslexia-Genetic aspects. In A. L. Benton & D. Pearl (Eds.), *Dyslexia: An appraisal of current knowledge.* New York: Oxford University Press.

Owen, F. W., Adams, P. A. Forrest, T., Stolz, L. M., & Fisher, S. (1971). Learning disorders in children: Sibling studies. *Monographs of the Society for Research in Child Development, 36* (4, Serial No. 144).

Pannbacker, M. A. (1968). A speech pathologist looks at learning disabilities. *Journal of Learning Disabilities, 1,* 403–409.

Pasamanick, B., Rogers, M. E., & Lilienfeld, A. M. (1956). Pregnancy experience and the development of behavior disorder in children. *American Journal of Psychiatry, 112,* 613–618.

Pennington, B. F., Bender, B., Puck, M., Salbenblatt, J., & Robinson, A. (1982). Learning disabilities in children with sex chromosome anomalies. *Child Development, 53,* 1182–1192.

Peters, J. E., Romine, J. S., & Dykman, R. A. (1975). A special neurological examination of children with learning disabilities. *Developmental Medicine and Child Neurology, 17,* 63–78.

Pincus, J. H., & Glaser, G. H. (1966). The syndrome of "minimal brain damage" in childhood. *New England Journal of Medicine, 275,* 27–35.

Plackett, R. L. (1964). The continuity correction in 2 × 2 tables. *Biometrika, 51,* 327–338.

Ramey, C. T., Stedman, D. J., Borders–Patterson, A., & Mengel, W. (1978). Predicting school failure from information available at birth. *American Journal of Mental Deficiency. 82,* 525–534.

Randles, R. H., & Wolfe, D. A. (1979). *Introduction to the theory of nonparametric statistics.* New York: Wiley.

Rapoport, J. L., & Zemetkin, A. (1980). Attention deficit disorder. *Psychiatric Clinics of North America, 3,* 425–441.

Reed, J. C. (1967). Lateralized finger agnosia and reading achievement at ages 6 and 10. *Child Development, 38,* 213–220.

Rie, E. D. (1980). Effects of MBD on learning, intellective functions, and achievement. In H. E. Rie & E. D. Rie (Eds.), *Handbook of minimal brain dysfunctions: A critical view.* New York: Wiley.

Rie, H. E. (1980). Definitional problems. In H. E. Rie & E. D. Rie (Eds.), *Handbook of minimal brain dysfunctions: A critical view.* New York: Wiley.

Ring, B. C. (1976). Effects of input organization on auditory short-term memory. *Journal of Learning Disabilities, 9,* 591–595.

Rodgers, B. (1978). Feeding in infancy and later ability and attainment: A longitudinal study. *Developmental Medicine and Child Neurology, 20,* 421–426.

Rosenberger, P. B. (1967). Visual recognition and other neurologic findings in good and poor readers. *Neurology, 17,* 322.

Ross, D. M., & Ross, S. A. (1976). *Hyperactivity: Research, theory, and action.* New York: Wiley.

Rourke, B. P. (1978). Neuropsychological research in reading retardation: A review. In A. L. Benton & D. Pearl (Eds.), *Dyslexia: An appraisal of current knowledge.* New York: Oxford University Press.

Rubin, R. A., & Balow, B. (1977). Perinatal influences on the behavior and learning problems of children. In B. B. Lahey & A. E. Kazdin (Eds.), *Advances in child clinical psychology.* New York: Plenum.

Rutter, M. (1970). Sex differences in children's responses to family stress. In E. J. Anthony & C. Koupernki (Eds.), *The child in his family.* New York: Wiley.

Rutter, M. (1978). Prevalence and types of dyslexia. In A. L. Benton & D. Pearl (Eds.), *Dyslexia: An appraisal of current knowledge.* New York: Oxford University Press.

Rutter, M. (1980). School influences on children's behavior and development. *Pediatrics, 65,* 208–220.

Rutter, M., Tizard, J., & Whitmore, K. (Eds.). (1970). *Education, health and behavior.* London: Longman.

Rutter, M., Tizard, J., Yule, W., Graham, P., & Whitmore, K. (1976). Research report: Isle of Wight studies, 1964–1974. *Psychological Medicine, 6,* 313–332.

Safer, D. J., & Allen, R. P. (1976). *Hyperactive children: Diagnosis and management.* Baltimore: University Park Press.

Satz, P., & Fletcher, J. M. (1980). Minimal brain dysfunctions: An appraisal of research concepts and methods. In H. E. Rie & E. D. Rie (Eds.), *Handbook of minimal brain dysfunctions: A critical view.* New York: Wiley.

Satz, P., Friel, J., & Goebel, R. A. (1975). Some predictive antecedents of specific reading disability: A three-year follow-up. *Bulletin of the Orton Society, 25,* 91–110.

Satz, P., Taylor, H. G., Friel, J., & Fletcher, J. M. (1978). Some developmental and predictive precursors of reading disabilities: A six-year follow-up. In A. L. Benton & D. Pearl (Eds.), *Dyslexia: An appraisal of current knowledge.* New York: Oxford University Press.

Schaefer, E. S. (1984, August). *Parent predictors of child adaptation: Implications for intervention.* Paper presented at the meeting of the American Psychological Association, Toronto.

Schain, R. J. (1977). *Neurology of childhood learning disorders* (2nd ed.). Baltimore: Williams & Wilkins.

Siegel, E. (1968). Learning disabilities: Substance or shadow. *Exceptional Children, 34,* 433–438.

Silver, A. A., & Hagin, R. A. (1967). Strategies of intervention in the spectrum of defects in specific reading disability. *Bulletin of the Orton Society, 17,* 39–46.

Strauss, A. A., & Lehtinen, L. E. (1947). *Psychopathology and education of the brain-injured child.* New York: Grune & Stratton.

Sulzbacher, S. I. (1975). The learning-disabled or hyperactive child: Diagnosis and treatment. *Journal of the American Medical Association, 234,* 938–941.

Swanson, H. L. (1979). Developmental recall lag in learning-disabled children: Perceptual deficit or verbal mediation deficiency? *Journal of Abnormal Child Psychology, 7,* 199–210.

Symmes, J. S., & Rapoport, J. L. (1972). Unexpected reading failure. *American Journal of Orthopsychiatry, 42,* 82–91.

Timm, N. H. (1975). *Multivariate analysis with applications in education and psychology.* Belmont, CA: Wadsworth.

Torgesen, J. (1975). Problems and prospects in the study of learning disabilities. In E. M. Hetherington (Ed.), *Review of child development research* (Vol. 5). Chicago: University of Chicago Press.

Torgesen, J. (1980). Conceptual and educational implications of the use of efficient task strategies by learning disabled children. *Journal of Learning Disabilities, 13,* 19–26.

Torgesen, J., & Dice, C. (1980). Characteristics of research on learning disabilities. *Journal of Learning Disabilities, 13,* 531–535.

Torgesen, J., & Goldman, T. (1977). Verbal rehearsal and short-term memory in reading-disabled children. *Child Development, 48,* 56–60.

Vellutino, F. R. (1977). Alternative conceptualizations of dyslexia: Evidence in support of a verbal-deficit hypothesis. *Harvard Educational Review, 47,* 334–354.

Vellutino, F. R. (1978). Toward an understanding of dyslexia: Psychological factors in specific reading disability. In A. L. Benton & D. Pearl (Eds.), *Dyslexia: An appraisal of current knowledge.* New York: Oxford University Press.

Vellutino, F. R., Steger, B. M., Moyer, S. C., Harding, C. J., & Niles, J. A. (1977). Has the perceptual deficit hypothesis led us astray? *Journal of Learning Disabilities, 10,* 375–385.

Versacci, C. J. (1966). *An epidemiological study of the relation between children's birth record information and reading achievement.* Unpublished doctoral dissertation, Temple University.

Wechsler, D. (1949). *Wechsler Intelligence Scale for Children.* New York: The Psychological Corporation.

Wender, P. H. (1971). *Minimal brain dysfunction in children.* New York: Wiley–Interscience.

Wender, P. H. (1973). Minimal brain dysfunction in children: Diagnosis and management. *Pediatric Clinics of North America, 20,* 187–202.

Werner, E. E. (1980). Environmental interaction in minimal brain dysfunctions. In H. E. Rie & E. D. Rie (Eds.), *Handbook of minimal brain dysfunctions: A critical view.* New York: Wiley.

Werner, E. E., Simonian, K., & Smith, R. S. (1967). Reading achievement, language functioning and perceptual-motor development of 10- and 11-year-olds. *Perceptual and Motor Skills, 25,* 409–420.

Werner, E. E., & Smith, R. S. (1977). *Kauai's children come of age.* Honolulu: The University Press of Hawaii.

Yando, R., Seitz, V., & Zigler, E. (1979). *Intellectual and personality characteristics of children: Social-class and ethnic-group differences.* Hillsdale, NJ: Lawrence Erlbaum Associates.

Zinkus, P. W., & Gottlieb, M. I. (1980). Patterns of perceptual and academic deficits related to early chronic otitis media. *Pediatrics, 66,* 246–253.

Author Index

K

L

M

N

O

P

R

Subject Index

U

V

W

DATE DUE